THE MATTER OF PERCEPTION

The Matter of Perception

A novel about manifesting a better life in the face of personal hardship

DENITA WALLACE

Grateful acknowledgment is made to
Malcolm MacGregor Photography for the cover photo
of the entrance steps to Percy Warner Park

First Printing, 2024

ISBN 979-8-218-31468-2

Foreword

For nearly a quarter century, I served as the Senior Minister of a small New Thought Church in Salem, Oregon. Denita Wallace was a member of my congregation—and so much more. Denita was and is my friend and served our church in every capacity. She was always there to assist when we called her and hollered "help". She exemplified compassion, understanding, and patience. When asked how she was on any particular day, Denita answered "fabulous, fantastic, or filled with joy." She was a delight to work with when she became my Office Manager. I could always count on Denita to boost my spirits and offer me a new perspective on a situation.

Over the years, Denita has taken numerous workshops and classes that have taught her about manifesting. And she has now written a book, which was a dream that has been hovering in the back of her mind for some years. When she mentioned this dream to me, I encouraged her to get started and trust the Universe to guide her through the process, which she has done.

Every time I would see Denita, since my retirement, I would inquire about the book's progress. She happily filled me in, and I was honored to read the first draft. Although writing a book can be difficult at times, Denita's happy, joyous attitude over the last couple of years has seen her to the completion of a wonderful story, filled with great wisdom.

Rev. Georgie Richardson

Chapter One

Summer 1985, Athens, Ohio

Mariah had finally tracked down Jack. It wasn't difficult; she and Jack had spent many weekend mornings here, but this was different. Even before reaching the door to Cafe Praline, she could already smell the delicious aroma of butter, chocolate, and browned sugar contrasted with the acid taste of fear in her mouth. She hadn't seen or heard from him in a week and a half, even though she'd left messages every day. It wasn't normal for him to be that way. Not in the entire four years they'd been a couple. Their relationship had settled into habitual patterns of dinner together, usually takeout, and then sitting on the couch to watch some television. Then Jack began to act differently. He often wanted to go out more and party but deferred to Mariah's wish to be a homebody, exactly the way she wanted it. Their time together was more sporadic, with days between their dates. And then, a week and a half.

Her fingers trembled as she reached for the long handle of the glass door. She felt nervous to be stalking Jack like this, but she needed to know what was going on. As a young couple walked up behind her, she stepped aside and let them enter first. Mariah followed behind and surveyed the crowded room as soon as the couple cleared her line of sight. The cafe had a quaint feel with mismatched tables and a hand-made wooden front counter. An ancient-looking espresso machine with pounded copper decorations stood next to the display case. The room seemed to rumble with the crowd of people stuffed in the small space, punctuated by an occasional high-pitched laugh and the *khwoooh* of the espresso machine. After a few minutes, she spotted Jack and Sandra sitting at a table, his pudgy hands wrapped around her bony fingers and, as far as Mariah could tell, looking into each other's eyes. Sandra? Confused, she started to move toward them, but then the two leaned against each other and kissed. Mariah quickly backed out of the café and scurried to her car. Feeling faint, she blindly pulled out of her parking spot and heard tires screeching and the blast of a car horn behind her. Bad idea to drive in this state. Panting, she returned to the parking place until able to get her head on straight. She finally made it home to her apartment where she sat staring into space, trying to think. It didn't make sense. Sandra—her best friend. Mariah and Sandra had met at their first job after high school. A nursing home had hired the two of them to clean rooms and bring food to the residents who couldn't come to the dining room. After leaving this temporary job, they stayed great friends, doing everything together. Four years ago, Sandra had introduced her boyfriend's best friend, Jack, to Mariah. It was fun going out as a foursome. The fact that Jack was patient, and didn't rush to intimacy relaxed Mariah, and they had gradually become lovers.

Why were Jack and Sandra holding hands and kissing? Deep down she knew the truth. The last time she had been with Sandra they'd talked about Mariah's frustration that she wanted to move her relationship with Jack to the next level. After dating for four years, something needed to change. And that change was a commitment—marriage. At thirty-one years old, she knew she hadn't much time left to start a family. And that's what she wanted more than anything—family. Mariah wanted their marriage to be like a partnership. She saw them hand in hand, going through life and managing the challenges along the way together. She'd imagined a life with Jack— having babies, raising children, taking them to kindergarten, going camping. Only it turned out that Jack didn't even like to camp.

Mariah had been leaving hints to Jack. She had talked with him about how they could save on rent if they lived together, and when he agreed, she insisted they would have to be married first. Now that she thought about it, Jack had been pretty resistant to the idea. Maybe he only thought of her as a convenient sex partner. Sure, their relationship seemed to be getting a little stale. So, did Sandra use that information to sabotage Mariah's relationship with Jack? Feeling doubly betrayed, Mariah was nauseous.

She paced around her apartment. Too many things reminded her of Jack. Lap blankets they shared while watching movies. She snatched them off her couch and noticed pieces of popcorn from two weeks ago. And under the cushions was more popcorn mixed with dirt and cat hair. She began to search out all the places where evidence of Jack still lurked. The extra towel in the bathroom. His old t-shirt, which still smelled of too-strong cologne. Spare toothbrush. Mariah threw everything into a big trash bag and took it out to the apartment complex's dumpster; then began vacuuming and cleaning the room. The activity enlivened her to give the entire apartment a thorough scrubbing. The clean apartment smelled better, but the room was still depressing.

She was now alone, and her head felt empty. She sat in her recliner, her ragdoll cat Sombra on her lap, then finally went to bed but couldn't sleep. More thoughts of what went wrong kept her awake long into the night. Should she have confronted Jack—or Sandra for that matter? But what's the point? Would confronting them change anything? Maybe it would make them feel guilty, which might help her feel righteously aggrieved. But it wouldn't help her a bit. Did she love him? Who knows? They had become so familiar with each other. Comfortable. This was Mariah's first long-term relationship and she had felt relieved to be out of the dating routine. Jack had chosen her, and she'd followed along. She didn't like going out with unknown men. She never knew what they wanted, and suspected it was only sex. Jack had been different. Respectful at first. After a while, though, his expectations had grown. Maybe Jack was also content with not having to go through the trouble of getting first dates but then wanted more than routine. At any rate, she should have seen this coming.

Monday morning Mariah overslept after tossing and turning all night, and then she didn't have time to work on her tangled hair. Showering and washing it would take too long drying and styling, so she just sponged off. Her eyes were puffy from sleep deprivation.

She was aware of some upheaval going on at work. Mike, the manager, was caught having an affair with his secretary, Kaylin. Mariah knew about the affair—everyone did— but thought it would all blow over soon. Besides, it didn't have to affect her since she wasn't involved in any way. Still, she didn't want to show up late. Rushing out the door, Mariah hit the stairs at breakneck speed. Halfway down, she stumbled as she shifted her body to make room for her neighbor, Bruce, on his way up.

"Easy there, filly," said Bruce, catching her by the waist and pulling her close to prevent her fall. They were now face to face. "You have the most gorgeous green eyes," he said, stroking a lock of her tangled auburn hair.

"I'm in a hurry," she said.

"How about getting together after work for some drinks?"

"Aren't you dating Bess?"

"We're not married yet," he said, winking. "Best time to look around."

Mariah turned so quickly that her hair slapped Bruce's face as she scampered the rest of the way down the stairs and to her car. "Arrrrgh! I hate that," she swore under her breath. "What is it about men? Are they all incapable of fidelity?"

At ten minutes past eight, Mariah arrived at work. She opened the door slowly hoping to slip in without many people noticing. Obviously, that would be impossible. A man she didn't recognize was posted at the door. Coworkers milled around looking stunned. She could see through the large window in Mike's office that he had cleaned out all his personal belongings. The desk and walls were bare, devoid of plaques and trophies. A man in the manager's office doorway stood staring at her. "Are you Mariah?" he asked.

"Yes, I'm sorry I'm late."

"Follow me. I need to talk to you."

Mariah walked into her old boss's office and sat in the only chair in front of the desk, her hands writhing in her lap.

"My name is Richard Preston. I'm sure you already know about the turmoil that has occurred here in the last few days."

"Maybe a little. About Mike and Kaylin?"

"Well, there's more to it than that," said Richard. "A lot more. Corporate has decided to close this office so we can sort out what's been going on. We're laying off everyone working here. Not that you have done anything wrong, as far as we know. Here's your check for your last month plus two months' severance pay. Go ahead and clean out your desk of personal items only," he said, handing her a box. "When you are ready to leave, our security officer will check out your box. Do not take any company items."

Mariah began sorting through her drawers. She only had a few personal things at her desk: a picture of herself and Jack at a company picnic, (which she would now be happy to pitch into the trash), a plastic ruler that she thought she'd brought from home, a moldy plastic spoon and carton from some old soup, and a paperback book she used to sneak out when business was slow. She stuck her purse in the box on the desk and headed to the restroom. Barbara was at the sinks, dabbing away the mascara running down her cheeks.

"That bad, is it?" Mariah asked.

"I'm just so angry. Mike and Kaylin have an affair and everyone in the office gets fired?"

"The guy said there was more to it than that. What else was going on here, some sort of embezzlement?"

"I do think it must have something to do with company finances, but I have no idea what."

Mariah put her finger toward her mouth. Barbara understood.

Mariah knew a little more than she had let on. She was aware that Mike had spent a lot of money on Kaylin. Keeping his own family and still supporting Kaylin the way he did would require much more cash than she thought Mike earned. Heck, he had even bought Kaylin a new car. Then she began demanding Mike get a divorce and marry her. Mariah and the other employees had witnessed yelling matches between Kaylin and Mike in his office. Mariah knew that it was a big mistake on so many levels to have a romantic relationship between a boss and an employee. It reinforced her resolve never to let herself fall into a situation like this.

As the receptionist, Mariah had also received some calls from clients complaining that their whole life account statements were wrong and looked dummied up. Could he have been pocketing the whole life insurance payments and then sending made-up statements? Mariah had figured it was none of her business at the time. Mike had a knack for making his employees feel threatened if they challenged anything he did. In a way, all this turmoil had made Mariah wish she could leave this place. Here was her chance.

When she got back to her desk, her box had been moved to the door and all the drawers had been opened and emptied. Mariah picked up the box, made sure her purse was in there, and walked past the "inspector" and out to her car. The crunching sound of churning gravel followed her as she gunned her car to the street. Then, out of habit, she drove to Café Praline. She had the place almost all to herself as she sat at a table with her pastry and coffee but found it difficult to eat. She'd shared too many mornings there with Jack. And her most recent discovery of Jack and Sandra, made her wonder why she even thought to come here. Her mouth was dry, and the food stuck in her throat. Besides, she had lost her appetite, so she headed home. Pulling away from Café Praline, a distracted Mariah switched on the radio and then grimaced. WRMR was playing "Physical"—still Jack's favorite song, even though it was three years old. She remembered how he would lean in and sing, "Let me hear your body talk, your body talk" as he grabbed her hair at the nape of her neck, oblivious to her mood at the moment. It became almost a game, one she disliked playing. Abruptly, she turned off the music. "At least I won't have to hear that asinine song again," she muttered.

As she opened her apartment door, she heard her phone ring. It was Abby, one of the mob she and Jack ran around with.

"What's up, Abby?"

"I'm calling to invite you to my party."

"Who's coming?"

"Oh, the usual group, Barbara, Sam, Jack and Sandra ..."

"Wait, what? You just said that like they're a couple."

"Well, they are a couple, you knew that, right?"

"No! Jack didn't even have the decency to break up after four years of dating. And I *thought* Sandra was my best friend, too. How could you just accept them as a couple? How long have you known about this?"

"That's sad, Mariah, I know how you must feel. I didn't know you didn't know, but I think everyone else knows. Surely you must have noticed how Jack always gravitated to Sandra when the group was together. Why don't you come to my party anyway? Maybe someone else will be there you'd like."

"I don't want to be a part of this group anymore. How could any of you be my friend and still accept Jack and

Sandra as a couple? I guess I just don't have friends." All those so-called friends came from Jack's side of the relationship anyway, except for Sandra.

"Mariah, you just need to let it go and move on. Holding a grudge will only prevent something good to come of it."

Hanging up, Mariah shook her head. Abby must think switching partners is totally normal.

She sat in shock. Everything she'd believed existed in her future had suddenly evaporated. She had no potential husband and, therefore no potential children. And no job to support her, either. In fact, she had no reason to stay in Ohio at all, and she grieved the miscarriage of her projected future. A low moan began deep in her belly and moved up to her diaphragm, becoming louder until it was a scream. With every new breath, she screamed louder, trying to purge the sick feeling of despair. Gradually, when she had nothing left inside, the screams reduced to sobs, and she cried herself to sleep.

Mariah wished she could take a long nature walk. In the past, strolling through the forest was one of her favorite ways to calm herself, but her apartment was nowhere near a forest, or even a little park. Sells Park was a thirty-minute drive and was one of her favorite places in the past, with all its mysterious rock formations and shady forest areas. She drove there and began to relax as soon as she had parked and started walking. The rhythm of her steps hypnotized her as she passed a green-scummed pond, the moisture-laden air pungent with a smell she knew from her childhood. Mariah was an only child of adventuresome parents. The MacKenzie family had done everything together. She had felt loved and protected by them and this is what she had wanted to create for herself. A loving family—a threesome unit with the safety and security of committed relationships.

How had she failed? One thing is for sure, she hadn't been to this park in years. She had gone along with whatever Jack had wanted to do, like going to baseball games. She had lost herself and wasted four years trying to fit that relationship into her dream.

Back in her apartment with time on her hands and nothing much to do, Mariah looked through the few books on her shelf. As her fingers moved absent-mindedly across the spines, they stopped at one—the book her parents had given her about manifestation. Carefully pulling it out, she blew off the dust and opened the front cover to read the inscription through the still-lingering dust cloud. *To our precious daughter, Mariah. May your life bring you all the happiness you desire.* Her parents were out of the country now. Their university sabbatical allowed them to travel to the Amazon to study a native culture. They had always been enterprising, eagerly moving ahead toward their desired goals. Mariah had rolled her eyes when she'd received the gift and put it away on the bookshelf, thinking the subject was too abstract and unrealistic to give any attention to. She had never read it, but maybe it was the very thing she needed. If nothing else, it would give her a feeling of closeness to her family, which she desperately wanted.

Sombra jumped into her lap as she curled up in a chair and started reading. The book seemed to be telling her she could manifest her dream, and that in fact, her dream could be even bigger than she'd ever imagined. She wondered how that was even possible. It went on to recommend she spend some time making her dream seem more real. The importance of a strong image of how it would look and feel prompted Mariah to pore through magazines for images that helped her focus her desires. The grocery store down the street had a big selection of magazines, so she spent the next few days looking through them. She found an article on Nashville, Tennessee. She bought it and a few other magazines to bring home and began to plan a strategy to manifest her destiny.

Nashville looked great. Photographs of the lush hills, lakes, and parks were especially enticing. That's where she'd go—Nashville. She would need to find a job and a place to live before even thinking about anything else. These goals in the manifestation book seemed pretty lofty. She couldn't even imagine what kind of job she could find quickly enough to get established in Nashville. She may as well figure on an entry-level position at first, like the receptionist job she'd had here at the insurance agency, and then move up later. It won't pay enough for a great place to live, but she'd keep her thoughts on just finding an affordable apartment. She still wanted a family but didn't know if that was ever going to happen. For now, she'd focus on the short-term plans. Mainly, the book recommended keeping a positive attitude and avoiding negative thinking. It'll be hard, but worth a try.

Mariah had to struggle to block out feelings of abandonment and despair over losing everything she thought she had going in Ohio, but focusing on a future in Nashville helped her move forward. Once she committed to move, she walked down to her apartment manager's office and put in her notice. The last month's deposit would cover her next month, so she would be able to hang on to the severance pay a little longer.

She began to look through her apartment and sort out what to take with her and what to sell or throw away. Luckily the grocery store had some boxes, and she began filling them with the few things she would bring. Books were too heavy, and she would sell them or give them away. All her furniture would go in a moving sale. She found herself fondling some of her old favorite stuffed animals and realized she couldn't just let them go. The old tiger had been a gift from her parents. The pink panther reminded her of the time she won it at the fair. Some of them had even survived her babyhood. They were like family. She lined them up in the back window of her old Ford Fiesta. She called the local newspaper to place an ad for her moving sale on the following Friday and Saturday. Mariah figured she needed every dollar she could get from her furniture and other stuff, so she ran individual ads for some of the furniture and bed frame in addition to the garage sale ad. She would have to repurchase everything when she found a place in Nashville. It will all work out, she thought, staying with the recommendation of her manifestation book.

Friday morning Mariah was ready. She had put handmade signs on the street corner and in front of her apartment. She'd moved everything she was taking into her car, which was stuffed to the roof with boxes and luggage, so anything left in the apartment was for sale. Garage sale shoppers marched in right at eight, but most were looking for knickknacks or small items. Close to the last hour on Saturday, a few people finally came back to barter on the furniture. She would call Goodwill to have them pick up the last unsold items. The wad of cash at the end of the sale would have to provide food and room on her trip.

Luckily, she had planned and put a little exercise mat in her car, where she could retrieve it without rummaging through the boxes. She unrolled it on the apartment's old brown shag carpet and spread a lightweight quilt to sleep. Sombra was restless. The poor kitty had only known this apartment since Mariah had adopted him as a tiny kitten. She was grateful for this black-and-white long-haired ball of fluff. Without his purr, sleeping would have been impossible.

Monday morning Mariah called Goodwill to pick up the items left from the sale. She spent most of the afternoon cleaning her apartment. She'd already packed the vacuum cleaner, so she had to unload and reload the car to pull it out. Sombra would need some sort of temporary litter box and a container to ride in. Mariah thought of using her day bag, a smaller piece of luggage that matched her larger suitcase. In case she found a motel that didn't allow pets, she could smuggle Sombra into the room in the bag, looking like luggage. To make it easier for Sombra to breathe, she cut a few holes in the bag. A cardboard carton would suffice as a litter box.

Mariah was ready to leave early Tuesday morning. She returned the key to the apartment manager, who followed her back to inspect. Satisfied with the cleaning, she gave Mariah a check for half the cleaning deposit.

Mariah headed to the gas station near the freeway, which had a little truck stop cafe beside it. The smell of gasoline added to the queasiness in her stomach making the decision to have breakfast difficult, but she told herself she had to eat something to settle her nerves as she headed into the unknown. The gingham-clad waitress served coffee and took her order for the advertised $1.99 breakfast of two eggs, hash browns, bacon, and toast. When it came, she played with the food on her plate while she nibbled at the toast with orange marmalade on it, which she had found fishing through the little packets of jam at her table. Piling the eggs on top of the hash browns, she cut into them so the yolks would leak into the potatoes. Then she crumbled the bacon onto the whole pile. By the time she finished her toast, her appetite had improved, and she ate the whole thing right down to scraping the last bit of yolky potatoes off the plate.

Driving away from Athens felt like driving off a cliff. Where would she even spend the night? Her destination was a huge black hole.

Chapter Two

Arriving in Nashville, Mariah took the first exit she saw with a Motel 6. It was not far off the highway, near a Mexican restaurant, and a pancake breakfast house. The shabby, ordinary box houses with ratty yards she passed didn't matter to Mariah. She expected to be there only a short while, hopefully, less than a week. She had a few hundred dollars in pocket money from the moving sale and a credit card. Her plan was to find a job before looking for a place to live. After checking into the motel, Mariah brought her suitcase and the matching grey bag up the metal outdoor staircase and into her second-floor room. Looking around, she noticed the stale smell of cigarette smoke still lingering on the bedspread and curtains. It was almost enough to make her gag, but she steeled herself to push ahead. A window overlooked the parking lot, and beyond it, the freeway, where she could hear the sound of downshifting trucks. She opened the small bag and gently pulled out Sombra. He head-bumped her arm and flopped down on the bed. Mariah began unpacking the items she would need to get started: one black jacket and skirt, a white blouse, and black shoes for job hunting. The rest were jeans, t-shirts, and colorful striped sneakers.

She put on jeans and her favorite teal t-shirt and headed out to find a restaurant and a newspaper. Mexican food did not appeal to her, so she resigned herself to the grocery store, where she found a long display counter with rows of cooked deli meat. Finally, she caught the clerk's eye.

"Canahelpyallw'somethi?"

Mariah had no idea what the woman said but assumed she could order. "I guess I'll take a quarter pound of the roast turkey."

"Wouyoulitha sliced?"

"Okay." Surely when they speak that slowly, they should be more understandable.

Mariah took the package and continued to walk around the store. A loaf of bread, some mustard and ketchup, a jar of sliced pickles, and a soda completed her meal. She stopped at the newspaper stand and picked up a copy of *The Tennessean*.

Back at the motel, she made herself a sandwich and plopped onto the bed with her newspaper. Job ad after job ad was either completely out of her interest or required some experience or expertise she didn't have. She thought she should probably look for a receptionist or secretary job since that's what she did before in Ohio. The trouble was, the many jobs listed in the paper didn't give her a sense of what the employers were like, or even what part of town they were in. Being brand new in Nashville, she wouldn't know where to start with them. Sombra made it difficult to read anyway and urged Mariah to put down the paper and pay more attention to him. She pulled him onto her chest, and he began to purr. "I'm trying to stay positive, Sombra, but to be honest, I wonder if I've made a terrible mistake."

Mariah wished she had someone to talk to, but the only people she would confide in were her parents and her best friend, Sandra, who was obviously no longer her confidant. She decided to wait and see what happens in the morning.

Before going to bed, Mariah brought the cardboard box from her car and put it in the closet. She opened a flap on one end leaving a hole for Sombra to enter the makeshift litter box.

The next morning, she pulled open the top of a single-serving container of cat food and set out a bowl of water. Luckily, Sombra always had a good appetite and consumed the whole tin. "I'll be back later, kitty." She put the Do Not Disturb sign on the outside door handle and headed to the nearby pancake restaurant for breakfast. The waitress introduced herself as Kathryn.

"Are you here for a meeting or vacation?"

"I just drove in from Ohio. I'll be looking for a job and moving here as soon as possible."

"Oh? What drew you to Nashville?"

"I can't say for sure. It just seems central. And I imagine there are plenty of things to do here."

"How true. Would you like some coffee?"

"I'd love some."

When the waitress came back with a whole thermal pot of coffee and poured the first cup, Mariah ordered pancakes and asked, "Is there a place around here that provides a mailing address? I've seen places where I come from that have boxes like a post office."

"We have a post office, of course."

"Well, the ones I was thinking of have a street address, and you can use that address and then have it say apartment whatever so it looks like you live there."

Kathryn cocked her head slightly to the right and shrugged.

It didn't take long for Mariah to give up on her pancakes. She guzzled the last of her coffee and headed downtown. A post office box is better than nothing.

She finally spotted a parking garage. The traffic prevented her from getting into the correct lane for the entrance, so she had to drive around the block. She finally found an open parking place on the third level. An elevator took her back down to the street. The area felt closed in and extremely business-oriented. Mariah wasn't sure where to start. The library was near, so she headed there. She found the directories and tried to look up a mailbox place and found nothing helpful, but she saw there was a post office nearby and walked to it. With a post office box number, she returned to the library. Entering through the big brass doors, she noticed a row of electric typewriters where she updated her resumé with the new address. *I just need to put out to The Universe for the perfect job*, she thought, as she sat down in a comfy, overstuffed chair. This led to an hour of resting, daydreaming, and downright procrastination. Hunger finally pulled her upright and out of the library, but where to? She felt so small and insignificant in this environment with businessmen hustling back and forth. Everyone seemed to have a certain drive. They all knew where they were going and why. Mariah wandered up one block, then down another without any specific purpose. She felt silly, like an impostor. She didn't belong there, prancing up and down the street in business clothes as if she had a job.

Across the street, a ten or eleven-story tall building had a sign in the front listing many different offices, and Mariah decided to scope it out. Inside, a small coffee and sandwich shop with a few tables and chairs provided a perfect place to plan what to do next. She took off her jacket and laid her briefcase on a chair. A line was already forming at the front counter. She stepped into it just as a rush of about ten other people lengthened it. Turning around slightly to check her things on the chair, Mariah heard someone speak.

"Are you new here? I don't think I've seen you here before."

"I don't know how to answer that," said Mariah. "I don't even work here, but I might like to. I'm just checking it out."

"What are you looking for?"

"Oh, just an entry-level receptionist job. I used to do that in Ohio."

Another woman piped in. "We have an opening for a temporary receptionist right now. Sorry, we haven't even introduced ourselves. I'm Dar and this is Sara. We work in a real estate attorney's office on the fourth floor. Do you want to come up with us and fill out an application?"

"Thanks, I'd like to."

Sandwiches in hand, the three women walked back to the tables, which by then had filled up except the one with Mariah's belongings. They sat down together to eat.

Sara wore her blouse unbuttoned at the top to show some cleavage, having a full figure without being obviously overweight. Her eyes, tastefully decorated with liner and eyeshadow, seemed to attract men whenever they passed her table. She tended to look around and follow them with her eyes, too, as if to check them out.

Dar's chiseled features and purposeful movements seemed to emit energy like a heat lamp. The intensity was tempered by a kindness in her voice. "Mariah," said Dar, "the front office secretary is about to have a baby and will be on maternity leave for the next three months. So, the job will be temporary, but openings often come up for other positions. We need to find someone immediately because so far, no one matches the job requirements. So many of the applicants are musicians or singers trying to make ends meet until they get discovered. Some of them couldn't even spell. One even wrote that her most relevant attribute was her great 'attion' to details!" All three women had a good laugh.

"The job sounds pretty much like what I was doing before at the insurance company," said Mariah, "so it should be a good fit."

After lunch, the three of them took the elevator to the fourth floor. Mariah saw Jackson & Verrone etched into the glass double door, right in front of the elevator. Just beyond was a reception area with a gray polished marble floor. Mariah was embarrassed at the squeak her soft-soled shoes made on the slick surface. The front desk stood at an angle on the back left side of the reception area, and on the right, a large opening led to the other offices. Dar introduced Mariah to Hannah, who stood up to shake hands. She was huge, as if ready to pop out twins. Hannah offered to make Mariah an appointment with Craig to interview for the job. Craig agreed to see her immediately and came right out. His slight build and super-curly head of hair made him look young, even though it was turning grey on the sides. Mariah thanked her new friends and followed him into his office. He sat behind his behemoth desk and began to read her resumé. "Your experience is adequate," said Craig. "I like the organized way you present yourself. One of the most important attributes we are looking for is attention to detail. It's good that you also separately listed your previous employment and references. How long have you known Dar and Sara?"

"About twenty minutes."

"Well, let me be honest with you. Hannah's last day is Friday. I need someone to come in and take over this job right away, and so far, none of the previous applicants were even close to what we needed. I can call a temp agency or hire you on the spot. Are you willing to audition for a few weeks? We can decide then if we want to go longer. And you know this is a temporary job until Hannah comes back, right?"

"Yes, Dar explained that to me. And I would like to audition."

"Okay then. I'll take you over to Martha, who will get all the paperwork straightened out, and then you can show up at eight o'clock Monday morning to start."

Mariah finished the paperwork. Sara and Dar had disappeared into the maze of hallways and doors, so she left the office.

Elated with the speed of her progress, Mariah was in a celebratory mood as she left the parking garage and headed toward the motel.

This was way easier than I had expected, she thought. *It proves that if you plan your life and follow through, you can make anything happen. I must be the queen of manifestation. I wonder if I agreed to the job too soon. Maybe there are better jobs I could have had. Should I have negotiated for more money? Should I apply for more jobs?*

By the time Mariah got to the motel, her emotions were a braid of disparate feelings—high over success interwoven with fear and insecurity, overlapped by downright depression and loneliness, which lapped back over the former in a swirling mess. The sky had begun to match those feelings as dark clouds formed, overlapping white ones, and finally building into an ominous darkness in the middle of the afternoon. Then lightning strikes predicted loud peals of thunder.

"Sombra, where are you? Kitty, kitty." Mariah had put the Do Not Disturb sign on the door and instructed the front desk that she did not want housekeeping services while she was there. Even so, she worried that someone might have opened the door and let Sombra out.

But there he was, under the bed, his two golden eyes peering from the darkness. The thunder was now more frequent and intense. Mariah dragged Sombra out and crawled back on the bed holding him tight. Although she was hungry, she had no interest in going out to look for food. She ate a few pieces of bread and went back to snuggle with Sombra.

When she awoke, it was morning. She headed over to the pancake house again, and this time opted for a big breakfast of eggs, bacon, and pancakes, hoping that would hold her until dinner. Kathryn wasn't there, but the new waitress was just as welcoming and friendly.

With the job already out of the way, Mariah spent the weekend exploring Nashville to get a feel for the neighborhoods and locate some cheap apartments. She grabbed a little apartments booklet and a map she'd found in the pancake restaurant. She had no idea what area she wanted to live in and, thumbing through the booklet, she started to worry that apartments in Nashville would be too expensive to rent on her temporary, low-paying job.

Driving around different parts of Nashville proved easier than she had expected. She found that the city was ringed by major roads and freeways making it possible to tour all the way around without getting too lost except for the fact that some of those roads changed names several times on their way around. The Cumberland River had a multitude of parks, and Mariah asked The Universe for someplace near a nice park for walks. Forested hills surrounded the city, so nature was easy to access. Mariah sucked in the sight of purple asters against green grass, the sounds of more birds than she could identify, and the damp, rich, earthy smells as if she had been starved for too long.

The parks reminded Mariah of when she was still living with her parents. Back then, they moved often. Sometimes the move was just due to their adventuresome spirit, and they camped out for weeks at a time in a teepee, a nod to her mother's Native American heritage. Other times they moved to a new university for her parents' degrees. Mariah was used to moving and was comfortable with it. She was perpetually the new girl in class as she went through public schools. It meant she never developed a deep, solid friendship with anyone when growing up, but she learned that no matter where she lived, she always found new friends who were quite a lot like her old ones. Perhaps the same would be true in Nashville. She liked Sara and Dar. Hopefully, they will become good friends.

Her weekend activities left her no closer to finding a place to live. Maybe Sara and Dar could offer some help on Monday. She didn't know where they lived, but they might know some cheap places. Best not to have to live in a teepee!

Chapter Three

Mariah had done receptionist work before but looking up phone numbers in the directory every time someone called did slow her down. And the office seemed more intense than it needed to be as if it was more about the workers' attitude than the amount of work getting done. People came and went at a pace that appeared to be frantically busy. Mariah kept up pretty well, considering it was her first day.

She did not, however, have time to check with Dar and Sara to see if they could join her for lunch. She was hoping to pick their brains about a place to live. When it was almost noon, Dar and a middle-aged woman showed up at Mariah's desk.

"Hi, want to go to lunch?"

"Yes! I was hoping to see you and Sara for lunch."

"Sara has a lunch date with someone else. This is Joyce. She'll sit at your desk while you're gone. Let's go."

Mariah and Dar bought their sandwiches and found a table in the cafe where they'd first met. Dar pulled off her jacket and hung it over the back of her chair. She was wearing a vertically striped, navy-and-white cotton knit shirt that made her lean body look even more striking. It made Mariah feel plump and frumpy by comparison.

"Well, how are things going on your first day?"

"All right, I guess. Once I memorize all the names and office extensions, it'll be a piece of cake."

"Wow. I'd say you are doing pretty well, then."

Mariah let out a deep sigh. "My biggest concern right now is finding a place to live. Do you have any ideas about a good location with reasonable rent?"

"Sara and I live in the same apartment complex just across the bridge on the east side. The rent might be a bit high for you, though." Then with a sudden jerk of her head, "Oh! Now that I think about it, one apartment in our complex *is* available. Someone just left. It's tiny and it hasn't been updated yet. It almost appears the building designer ended up with some leftover space and just tried to squeeze in one more unit, kind of like an afterthought. It's right in the corner, so at least it gets light from two sides. I'll bet the manager would be happy to get that one rented right away since she's been busy updating some other units right now. After work, why don't you come with Sara and me to our place and we'll talk to her?"

"Great!"

With a puzzled look, Mariah asked, "You and Sara seem to have a close relationship, and yet you seem so different from each other."

"I think it's just a matter of mutual respect."

"You mean about your work?"

Dar tipped her head with a half-smile, leaning forward to speak more softly. "Something most people don't realize is that Sara is a genius. Honestly. She has a photographic memory. She remembers everything. She's also a whiz at math. There's almost nothing you could ask of her that she couldn't just do in a snap—things that would take the rest of us ten times as long. She has more free time than the rest of us because she's so quick and efficient. That means she has time to flirt with the men in the office, so it might seem like she's not working much. I, on the other hand, have to work hard all the time to achieve what I want. I'm taking classes while I work here at J & V, trying to get my law degree. And I run. I'm preparing for a half marathon."

"Wow, Dar, that's quite a lot. Can't you cut back on something, like the half marathon?"

"Actually, running calms me down. If I didn't run, I'd be too uptight. And the training for the half marathon is just to keep me on schedule. It's all for my mental health."

When the workday finally ended, Mariah followed Dar's directions to the apartment complex. The drive across the bridge was harrowing to Mariah, with cars switching between multiple lanes. The trucks never slowed down for anyone. She wondered if she would be able to survive the commute every day. Dar and Sara were standing on a balcony overlooking the entrance so they could spot Mariah as she drove in. "Up here," they both yelled. Mariah found the metal stairway with concrete steps, which echoed the sound of her feet like thumping a watermelon as she climbed to join them.

Because Dar had already told the manager about Mariah, they immediately went to look at the empty apartment. It was indeed small. It hadn't been cleaned yet and smelled like dirty socks. The carpets had a few stains. The sinks and toilet had rust smears and the linoleum tiles on the bathroom floor were pulling up. The manager rambled on about how she didn't have time to deal with cleaning an empty apartment, and how the tenant was supposed to have left it clean.

"If I did the cleaning myself," Mariah asked, "would you waive the cleaning deposit?"

After some back-and-forth regarding the rent price, Mariah put down first and last and took immediate possession of the apartment with the key. Dar and Sara invited Mariah to join their carpool to work. This meant Mariah could save money on gas and parking fees, which was a huge financial benefit and a relief not to have to brave that drive by herself.

She let the motel know she'd be checking out the next morning. The rest of the week Mariah slept on the exercise mat she'd had the foresight to bring. She spent every evening cleaning walls, floors, kitchen cabinets, and, of course, the bathroom. On Friday night, Dar and Sara commented on the dark circles around Mariah's eyes.

"I have to shop garage sales this weekend—especially for a bed," she said with a rueful smile.

Sara crossed her arms. "I wouldn't buy a used bed. You can't know what kind of bedbugs and spiders would be in there."

Mariah laughed as she sprawled out on the floor. "I'm great at manifesting. That's why I got this job on my first day in town. And now I already have an apartment. With the right planning and some intuition, I can get anything."

Dar raised her eyebrows and with a wry smile said, "Really."

Mariah startled when she realized the implication of what she had said. "Oh, I didn't mean to minimize the help from you two. I appreciate all you've done for me. I'm so grateful you even spoke to me that day at the cafe. Your friendship means a lot to me."

"It's not a problem," answered Dar. "Where did you get these ideas about manifestation?"

"I read about it in a book called *Getting What You Want*, or something like that." It's an ancient book passed down to me from my parents. They were always moving to new places, and then they got into this self-help stuff. Later they became university professors and now they're on sabbatical in some South American jungle to work with the natives. They're real adventure-seekers."

"Back to the bed," Sara said. Both Mariah and Dar laughed until they were rolling on the floor. "No, seriously. Don't you think you could at least buy a new mattress? Then you could get the bed frame from a garage sale."

"Well, I'll think about it, I don't know what I'll find. I'm still worried about running out of money, so the cheaper I can find things, the better," Mariah mumbled.

Mariah didn't have a plan. On Saturday she drove around looking at garage sales without finding anything useful until she came across a church having a huge yard sale. She walked through the church lawn. Long tables were strewn with dishes, knickknacks, and toys, yet none of the furniture she sought. A squat lady with grey hair tied in a bun approached her. "Can I help you find anything?"

Mariah sighed, "Well, unless you can help me find a bed, a dresser, a sofa, and a dining table, probably not."

The woman looked at Mariah for a long time as if sizing her up. Still looking deep in thought, she told Mariah to stay there and disappeared into the church building. After about fifteen minutes, which felt like an eternity of wasted time, the woman came back out with a smile. "One of our parishioners recently died. Her family had just purchased a hospital bed as she was starting hospice. She never got a chance to sleep in it before she died. The bed and furniture in the house will be donated to the church and we could sell it to you. They will just have to get someone with a truck to bring it all over to the church later today."

A hospital bed? Odd, but the mattress would be new. Mariah hesitated. "Well, could the truck driver just bring it straight to my apartment? And how much do you think the whole thing would cost?"

"You'll have to make us an offer. We can't tell you what to pay. What were you planning to spend for all these items?"

Mariah was afraid to name a price. What if they say no? What if the offer exceeds what they were wanting? Finally, Mariah came right out with it. "I had budgeted three hundred dollars, but I wasn't counting on a brand-new bed. Can you work with that figure?"

The woman left again and went into the church. After yet another fifteen minutes, she came back and said yes. One of the men running the sale said he and another young man could go get the furniture. Mariah gave him her address and paid the woman. She was now the proud owner of an apartment full of furniture, sight unseen.

At six that evening, the furniture arrived, and the two men hauled it up to Mariah's second-floor apartment. After they left, she examined her new possessions. Her shoulders slumped as she noticed the permanent dips in the sofa cushions, which were a faded brown, green, and orange floral design that would definitely need a slipcover—or even just anything. The dining table had metal legs and a metal rim around a Formica top. Of the three chairs, two had split seats. The wooden dresser was small with only three draw-ers. At least there was the new bed. The mattress was still covered with plastic.

Later, as soon as she took the cover off, Sombra jumped up on the bed. Hmm, a feline seal of approval. Mariah used the crank on the side to raise the head of the bed. Smiling, she imagined leaning back comfortably, snuggled up with Sombra and a book.

On Sunday, Mariah invited Dar and Sara over to her apartment to see how she did with the garage sales. She'd bought some cheese and fancy crackers and a bottle of wine. Sara offered to bring her wine glasses. Mariah showed the two women around the apartment, proudly announcing the brand-new hospital bed. Sara laughed. "Are you planning to be sick?"

"No, but look how I can crank it up to comfortably read in bed."

"And how you don't plan on having a man over for sex," said Sara.

After toasting her furniture haul, Sara asked Mariah about her manifestation talent. Mariah shared what she'd read about visualizing her goals and trusting the process. She also mentioned that you had to be ready to receive the things you want and eliminate any negative thoughts.

"No offense," said Sara, "but if you can manifest what-ever you want like that, then why did you settle for this? Why didn't you go for a higher-paying job?" Her arm swept around the apartment. "And a nicer place with new fur-niture?"

"This is just the beginning. I didn't think I could realisti-cally get everything all at once, so I started with just getting a basic job and apartment. Next, I'll be thinking about finding a better job before this one ends. What I really want is a good job, a nice place to live, and a family—complete with a loving husband."

Sara squeezed her brows together. "Do you honestly think you can control life down to each detail by your thoughts? Does that leave room for the random events of life or even other people's thoughts?"

Dar broke in, "But all that you've accomplished in this short time is amazing—a job, an apartment, furniture, and a brand-new bed in just a week. I think most people would have taken a long time to get to this point."

After they left, Mariah felt let down. First, she thought Sara was being nasty to her. *Why did she have to be so critical? Who does she think she is? Her goal seems to be sleeping with the handsomest, high-status lawyer she can land. If she's such a genius, isn't she wasting her genius on sexual adventures? Although, her talent for picking up men could be useful in finding a husband.... But maybe Sara was right. This apartment and the furniture aren't much to be proud of. Why not make a bigger statement to the world? Of course, one has to be fiscally responsible. What would it take? Knowing how, maybe. Sara and Dar both seem to have their sights on bigger things. Dar is taking night classes and planning to become an attorney. She wants to be a partner in a law firm someday. It makes sense to at least try to move up in this company and get paid more. And before Hannah comes back! And what about dating?* Mariah wasn't sure where to start. Dating random new men didn't appeal to her at all. It seems like single men her age just want to jump into bed on the first date. She wasn't afraid of sex. She just wanted a relationship a lot deeper than that, and she thought having sex right away somehow blocked a developing relationship. How does one go about finding an unmarried man who wants to marry and have children? Do they even exist? If so, where would they be found? Maybe already married.

Chapter Four

The car was weaving through traffic at an uncomfortable speed. They were not running late, but Dar seemed to feel impatient with the rate of traffic in general. She was skilled at maneuvering through the cars and trucks. Mariah would have been overwhelmed by the pace and seeming rudeness of the other drivers.

Mariah shifted over behind Dar so that she could talk to Sara in the front passenger seat. "Tell me more about what you do at Jackson & Verrone," she yelled.

Sara stared ahead for a while before she began to speak. "We work with the documents for different real estate transactions. Sometimes we just have to organize the documents to get them ready for a closing. We check them and make sure we have all our ducks in a row. We also manage timelines—when to order an inspection or make sure a site plan is ready for approvals, things like that."

"What skills and education are required for that work?" Mariah asked.

"Well, no degree or anything, but you need to know the documents in a real estate closing. And you must spot mistakes in some documents, such as charges in the mortgage and all. Our job is to make sure we have everything we need before a closing. And we check the contract to confirm all the contingencies are satisfied. But you can learn all that by taking some courses through real estate companies.

"That's what I want to do," declared Mariah. "I've decided that's my new manifestation goal."

Sara shrugged. "Shouldn't be too hard to manifest that one."

Mariah wondered if Sara was being snarky again but said nothing. As soon as she got to work, she borrowed a brochure from Sara and started scoping out course offerings. Real Estate Financing Options sounded hard but was the next one available, so she signed up immediately. The class was to start on Saturday morning. It made her nervous in some ways but excited as well. Working toward a new goal gave her a sense of controlling her destiny. It wasn't too expensive, either and she had enough room on her credit card.

On Friday, Hannah came into the office with her new baby, Brendon. A knot of people came to the front to see the baby, and Hannah wanted to go back to talk with some of her friends, so she let Mariah hold Brendon and trotted off. Mariah held the baby for a while and marveled at the tiny, perfect features. He had long fingers with microscopic nails. She put her finger against Brendon's hand, and he curled his fingers around hers. Mariah held him up to her shoulder and Brendon turned his head toward her chin and tried to suck on it. It felt like kisses. For a moment, Mariah fantasized about what it must be like to have a little being like this—to raise children, to experience all the stages of family life. Hannah came back for Brendon, leaving Mariah thinking about babies and how she'd expected to be starting a family by now. That yearning built stronger in her until it stung, knowing she had no reason to hope at this point she could have it for herself—at thirty-one and still without a man, maybe too late.

With her mind still on Hannah's return, now in six weeks, she went to Craig to ask what other steps she would need to take for an attorney's assistant job like Dar's and Sara's. Craig said Mariah had shown herself to be dependable, capable, and accurate in her work. He offered to let her do some of the filing that would be a part of the job she was seeking. She could do this in her spare time. She thanked Craig and left feeling hopeful that she was progressing toward a promotion.

Mariah found the two-story brick building for the real estate class and climbed the stairs to the classroom. Inside, about ten people milled around in clusters. Some of them looked like they knew each other and nervously clung to familiar participants. Mariah set her things on the plastic table in front of an empty chair. Caterers brought in a large urn of coffee, hot water, and a tray of sweetener, creamer, and Styrofoam cups. Although Mariah had loved the coffee at Café Praline, coffee in urns wasn't her thing. It did make the room smell better, though.

Once the class was about to start and people began sitting, one of them walked up to the front of the class and introduced himself as Mr. Hansen. He wore khakis and a colorful print short-sleeve shirt. His sandy hair and clear blue eyes that you could look right through as if they were an open window, gave him a boyish appearance. Mariah thought he might be in his mid-to-late thirties. He passed out class materials to the participants and asked them what they hoped to get from being in the class. Then he gave an overview of the subjects he would be covering.

"With interest rates as high as thirteen percent," he said, "we all need to be proficient at finding creative ways to help buyers get into the home of their dreams. Imagine you are working with a couple who are veterans. They have $40,000 in a regular savings account getting four percent interest. They also have $70,000 in a CD at eight percent with a penalty for early cash-out. They want to buy a house that currently has a VA assumable loan of $55,000 at eight percent interest. The asking price of the home is $95,000. These people ask you to help them decide if they should put their entire liquid savings into a down payment and assume the VA loan, keep their savings account and borrow against their CD, or negotiate with the sellers to wrap the VA loan into a seller financing arrangement at ten or twelve percent interest if the seller were willing. The goal of this class is to help you to know where to start with this couple to analyze their situation and guide them through the best choices."

Mariah had never thought of herself as a math whiz, but she found the challenge to be downright exciting. Most of the men in the class acted like they already knew the material, but underneath the façade, she could see they were confused and refused to admit it. The four other women in the class all moaned as if finance was impossible to comprehend. One of the women bolted out the door and didn't come back. Mariah understood that either attitude would sabotage her learning, so she worked with the concepts and asked questions when she needed clarification. Mr. Hansen patiently answered her questions.

At noon, most of the group left the classroom to find lunch. Mariah had brought hers and decided to eat it there.

Mr. Hansen was still in the room and sat down next to her. "How's the class going for you so far?"

"I love your stories. They make the material seem relevant and interesting. I never knew this kind of math could be so inspiring."

"Well, thank you for that. It's part of my mission to inspire new people into this business."

"I wish I could be one of them, but I wouldn't be able to do something like that. I understand I would only be paid after closing on a house sale. How long would that take? I need a steady income to live. I wonder how people can afford to get started in real estate."

"People find all sorts of ways to get started in this business," he said. "Some have a spouse who can sustain them in the beginning. I even had a couple get up at three o'clock in the morning to throw newspapers for extra income."

At the end of class, Mr. Hansen concluded the lesson and asked everyone to clear out as quickly as possible so he could close up. As Mariah opened her car door to leave, she caught a glimpse of Mr. Hansen practically running out to his car and driving off. She wondered what the urgency was about.

With one more weekend for this class, Mariah took the study materials home. The fancy Hewlett-Packard finance calculator that Sara had loaned her had a strange entry order for calculations. It was backward from an intuitive way of inputting a calculation. Mr. Hansen had said Texas Instruments had a new calculator out with a more straightforward entry and it even cost less. Mariah returned Sara's calculator and bought the new TI one for herself. She brought it home and did the calculation examples from the class materials over and over just to gain familiarity with her new instrument.

As she was finishing the second weekend of class, Mariah made some new friends. She had several conversations with Mr. Hansen. He even sat with Mariah at lunch again. She told him all about how she had come to Nashville with no job or place to live and got both in the first week. He shared interesting stories about real estate challenges he had overcome. Mariah fantasized about what a wonderful career real estate would be, but she knew it would be impossible to get a start without funding. Two people in the class were also getting their licenses under Mr. Hansen, and they encouraged Mariah to do the same. She thought it could be a good idea, so she signed up for the pre-license class, which covered real estate law, geometry for measuring houses, and much more. It would be useful for her promotion at Jackson & Verrone, as well. The class was longer and more expensive, but something inside made her feel it would be worth it. Besides, Mr. Hansen was a delightful teacher with the perfect blend of teaching skills and an all-around-good-guy personality. When she finished the training, she would take the exam—just in case the license ever came in handy.

The next month flew by as Mariah settled into the routine of working while keeping her sights on the promotion. In the car on the way to work, she asked Dar and Sara what else she should do toward this goal. Sara was the first to address Mariah's image. "You should think about what you wear and how you comport yourself."

"How do you mean?" asked Mariah.

"Start with clothes. You need to get another nice suit. The skirt length is wrong in the one you're wearing. And you need to be in four-inch-high heels."

Mariah was confused. "Why?"

"Lots of reasons. For one, they make you taller. That means you can look men straight in the eye. And it changes your posture, too."

Mariah sneered, "Yeah, I've seen how it makes you sway your hips."

Sara laughed. "That's not the shoes. Just look at all the other women in the office and see how they dress. There is a reason for it."

Dutifully, Mariah went shopping the next weekend for new clothes. She had studied all the women who came into the office and convinced herself that Sara was right. Even Dar, who was so straightforward and no-nonsense, dressed the same way. Plus, those high heels didn't squeak on the polished marble foyer.

The heels were hard to get used to. They did change her posture and she needed some coaching from Dar and Sara on how to carry herself with authority. She hired a seamstress to alter her new forest green suit skirt to the current fashion at the top of her knee. She had her old suit altered to fit her better and the skirt, which had been mid-calf, shortened to just above the knee.

It was getting close to the time Hannah would be back, and the office was abuzz with a big contract for one of the newer attorneys. He had landed a large project with housing and commercial properties all on one land parcel. It would require a lot of manpower. Sara was excited, as the new attorney was single and cute. She figured she could work into a supervisor position and maybe "main squeeze" as well.

Craig called Mariah back to his office. "Hannah will be returning in two weeks. I like your work ethic, your attention to detail, and your desire to take on more. Are you interested in working on the new project?"

"Of course," blurted Mariah.

"I'll start you with some filing and organizing to begin with and then, as you gain more experience, we can add some of the technical aspects. This work will be by billing hours. The hourly pay will be more than you are making now but might be more sporadic. Is that acceptable?"

Mariah paused a minute before saying yes.

"One more thing," said Craig. "We need you to start getting the files set up next week, even though Hannah will not be back yet. Would you be willing to work in the evening during that overlap week?"

"Hmmm," said Mariah. "Would there be any extra pay for that? Like overtime or a bonus or something? It will mean I have to drive to work with my own car and pay for parking and such."

"How about if I give you a parking garage pass for the week?"

"Okay, I'll go with that."

The week sped by as Mariah worked all day, had a quick bite, and came back to organize the new filing system for the upcoming project. Once home, she flopped down on her hospital bed after feeding Sombra. Then the two curled up together and immediately fell asleep without even moving.

Until Friday, that is. Maybe it was the long hours four days in a row, or perhaps the phase of the moon, but Mariah felt like a klutz all day. In the middle of the day, she walked down the hall past Dar, who pulled her aside. "Did you see your stockings?"

"No, what?" Mariah looked down. It was a huge run in her black nylons about an inch wide going all the way up her leg. Being pragmatic, she decided to take them off and go bare-legged. Then she tripped on the carpet and skinned her knee. Now everyone who passed her stared at her knee, which caused her to feel terribly self-conscious. Mariah just wanted this day to be over and dreaded another several hours of work.

If Mariah was anything, she was reliable. Never mind that she was tired, disheveled, and wanted to go home. She was determined to complete the after-hours filing. She started right after work, skipping dinner entirely. In her new work-station, she saw a note.

> *Mariah—We need to separate all the files for the commercial jobs from the condos and zero lot lines. Each job needs its own file and within each file, there should be several sub-files for permits and approvals, orders, etc.*

That's not how they had previously told her to do it!

It would take many hours to sort out all the components for each job. Mariah wondered if this new position was even right for her. She felt uncomfortable with how she dressed and the pace at the office. By eleven she'd had all she could take and decided to clock out and go home.

She was feeling shaky as she left the building and crossed the street toward the garage. The sidewalk was uneven, and she stumbled a few times as she wobbled in her four-inch heels. Her stockingless feet were clammy from sweat and they slipped in the shoes, exaggerating the wobble. One of those stumbles knocked off the end of her heel and the remaining shaft made a loud striking noise as she walked on the sidewalk. A blinking streetlight annoyed her further. She was almost to the parking garage when it flickered and then went out entirely. She was in darkness.

Chapter Five

Arthur lay in a drunken stupor behind a lamppost next to the parking garage. In one hand he clutched a brown paper bag with an empty whiskey bottle. He was stewing in anger. His boss, Cassie, had berated him in front of the whole office. Nothing he did was right for her. Arthur had tried to do everything she'd asked him to do—from distributing the mail to hand delivering packages to changing the water in the cooler. Sometimes Cassie would even send him out to buy her cigarettes. That afternoon she had lit into him about the water cooler. He'd tried to change the carboy, but it slipped out of his hand and broke on the floor. Water mixed with shards of broken glass splayed out in every direction. He quickly went to the janitor's closet to pull out the mop and bucket, along with a broom and dustpan for the glass. The women in the office were already complaining loudly about the mess. He spent over an hour trying to sop up five gallons of water plus the broken glass. Finally, after he'd cleaned up, Cassie stomped up to him, making an annoying *tack tack* sound with her spike heels. Grabbing his arm, she pulled him into her office where she handed him a final check. "Don't come back," she hissed, shoving him out the door.

He stumbled out of the office and down the street. Arthur wasn't much of a drinker, but he headed to the nearest liquor store and bought a fifth of cheap whiskey. He spent the remainder of the afternoon wandering around the city, lamenting that he was such a sad sack. Memories of cruel treatment from his boss, mother, and sister, Nilda flooded his mind one after the other. Nilda had been the worst, constantly berating him and calling him a loser. He cried. He screamed. But nothing gave him peace. By night-time, he lay near a flickering streetlight, which made his surroundings seem even more surreal.

Arthur knew only one person who had dominion over the women in his life—his father, Gregor. The women in his family feared him. He got angry over the smallest thing. Yelling would eventually turn to physical violence. When Arthur was three, he watched his father get mad at the housekeeper (Arthur's favorite person at the time) and hit her so hard she screamed. He'd grabbed her, pushed her down against a chair, and pulled up her skirt. He'd kept bumping against her over and over. She'd struggled, then whimpered, then gotten quiet with a stony stare into nowhere. When it was over, she'd left crying and never returned.

The empty whisky bottle lay beside Arthur under the lamppost. He was finished being pitiful. His sadness had turned to anger and hate. Now Arthur's fury was so strong that all he could feel was the hard pounding of his heart. It made his kidneys throb. His hands were tight fists.

Then, on the lonely street, he heard a sound. *Tack tack tack*, reminding him of his earlier experience with Cassie. He held his ears. No good. The sound was hammering a nail into his head. He had to make it stop. By now the sound was closer and he could see it was attached to a woman. He struggled to get up, holding the lamp post. The streetlight went out entirely. *Tack tack tack*. He lunged at the figure. Both fell forward with a disgusting crunch as they hit the ground: Arthur on top, his hands pinned under the woman's waist, blood seeping from her head.

Arthur was confused. Anger and fear were at war in his mind. He struggled to free his tangled arms and legs, but it was like wrestling with a blanket during a nightmare. Groping his way free, he found her bare legs. Then, in the most brutal way a man can demean a woman, he pulled open his trousers and shoved himself into her again and again until he released the tension of his anger and hatred. Leaving the woman bleeding on the sidewalk, Arthur tried to run, but he couldn't get far. The urge to vomit led him to a large bush behind a building and he crawled underneath it. Fearing the police, he stayed in the bush, curled up tightly the rest of the night.

Two policemen were making their last round when they slowly drove their cruiser past the parking garage. "What's that?" yelled the officer riding shotgun, pointing at the figure sprawled on the sidewalk. The driver pulled over abruptly. The two officers jumped out and ran to the woman. As one called for an ambulance, the other felt for a pulse.

"She's still alive."

"Good," his partner responded and immediately began searching for evidence. But aside from an empty fifth in a paper bag, he came up short. Donning gloves, he picked up the bottle and walked around the general vicinity but could find no footprints or disrupted grass. When the ambulance arrived, EMTs placed the victim inside and took off with sirens wailing and lights flashing.

The officers were about to follow the ambulance when an urgent call came over the radio ordering them to go immediately to the All Comers nightclub. Someone had just fired shots, killing three people and injuring a dozen others. With their own lights ablaze, the policemen responded to the call.

Arthur awoke with the sun shooting daggers through the branches of an overgrown rhododendron where he lay. His vomit, three inches from his head, smelled like rotten milk laced with booze.

His head in a vise, he slowly eased himself out of the bush. What had happened? Something made him fear the police, but what? He had been hiding but couldn't remember why. Realizing they might still be searching for him, he ventured out warily, scanning for any sign of law. He knew of a nearby park with a water fountain, so he headed that way. After washing his face and hands, he checked his body for any sign of blood. None that he could see. His pants were muddy and wrinkled, and his shirt reeked of vomit. Knowing he couldn't take the bus in that condition, he walked the five miles to his home, taking the back streets.

Arthur's place was a tiny, converted shed behind a house surrounded by a chain link fence. He unlocked the padlock securing the gate and went into his one-room studio. A one-piece counter with a sink, a small under-counter fridge, and a built-in, two-burner stove occupied one wall. His bed, a four-drawer dresser, and a small table took up the rest of the room. Collapsing into bed, Arthur slept for nineteen hours.

He awoke when the room got too hot to sleep any longer. He stripped off the stinking, rumpled clothes and squeezed into his tiny shower. Dressed in clean clothes, Arthur ventured into the backyard and sat on a retaining wall to think. He tried to sort out what had happened. Disjointed images came and went. He remembered leaving his job after being fired. He remembered Cassie yelling at him. What had he done that got her going? Oh yeah, the broken water bottle. In his mind, he saw persistent images of violence and rape. Sometimes he remembered his father raping the maid. And sometimes he was doing the raping. Was it just his imagination? Had he actually done this? In his drunken state the night before, he couldn't be sure what had happened, but something had made him afraid of the police.

Luckily, his rent was low and partially subsidized by the landscape maintenance work he did around the house, so he had sizable savings to tide him over. Arthur worked the rest of the morning deadheading the roses and peonies and weeding the beds. While he was at it, he picked some purslane out of the weed pile, went around through the back gate to the alley, and found some more to add to his dinner. That afternoon, he walked to the grocery and bought a newspaper. Did it have anything about the night before last? He didn't remember much after buying the whisky, but the uneasiness wouldn't go away and the police . . . a column or two had a follow-up story about a shooting at All Comers. Arthur wondered if he should try to find yesterday's paper but couldn't.

The renters in the main house were moving out. Friends were helping them, and all day a constant stream of people came and went. They laughed and yelled out to one another as if the move were a big party. By evening, he could hear the vacuuming and cleaning, and then they were gone.

Arthur welcomed the quiet. He needed more time to think. Why did he feel so much dread? What could he have possibly done? His father kept coming to mind. What did it have to do with his father? And where could he find a new job? He went back into his apartment and slept some more.

Chapter Six

Mariah tried to open her eyes. She felt as if heavy weights were pushing down on her head. She could hear some sounds, mostly people mumbling. For a while, she tried to figure out what they were saying, but it was too difficult, and she fell back asleep.

Then someone came into the room and spoke. "Hi, would you like someone to talk to?" Mariah's eyelids were still too heavy. "Would you like me to sing to you instead?" She sang like an angel. Before long, Mariah had a smile on her face. She struggled to move her mouth and coordinate her breathing to say thank you. She finally opened her eyes, but the angel was gone.

Two nurses walked in.

"Here she is! Eyes finally open. Looks like she's back to the living!" one of the nurses shouted. They began checking tubes and dials around Mariah. One tried to peek under the bandage on Mariah's head, which was covering a tube.

"Ow!" cried Mariah.

The nurse quickly apologized. "If you're in a lot of pain, we can fix you up with a morphine drip. I'll be back in a bit."

"Wait! How long have I been here? What happened to me?"

The nurse replied, "We have many questions for you, too."

The two nurses left. The room felt slightly cold and smelled antiseptic. Mariah noticed tubes attached to her arm. Instruments on both sides of her bed made various humming sounds as they monitored her status.

Two hours later the nurses came back with a doctor and another drip pole. As one of the nurses connected it to the tube in Mariah's arm, she said, "This one has morphine in it. Here's a button you can push for more morphine whenever you are in pain."

The doctor examined Mariah's head and then left with one of the nurses. Turning to Mariah, the other nurse said, "Now we can talk. My name is Petra. To start with, we need to know who you are. We found some information but need to verify it. What is your name? What's your address? Where do you work?"

Mariah answered the nurse's questions one by one, informing Petra that her parents were out of the country and could not be contacted. Then she began asking her own questions. Petra answered with what she knew.

"You were brought here in an ambulance that the police had called. The ambulance driver told us you'd been found lying face down on the sidewalk. They didn't know any details of what happened to you. We expected the police to come in and give us some information and also ask you some questions, but they didn't show up, probably because of the shooting that happened the same night." She continued gently, "We did take a rape kit sample because you had a lot of bruising in that area, and you had nothing on under your skirt."

"Well, actually I didn't have anything on under my skirt because of a little problem I had earlier," Mariah admitted.

"That doesn't make any difference," said Petra. "The results indicate that if you hadn't had sex earlier in the evening, it does appear you were raped."

"Oh." After a pause, Mariah added, "I hadn't had sex."

She and Petra fell silent

"So," sighed Mariah, "you don't know if they caught the guy?"

"We don't know anything."

"How long will I be here?"

"It depends on how you're healing. We're concerned about your head—your brain. We kept you in a coma for a few days while we tried to hold down the swelling."

"A few days!"

Mariah didn't like the idea of taking morphine, but the pain in her head was unbearable. The morphine barely took the edge off. Maybe she wasn't pushing the button often enough. However, the morphine caused her mouth to be so dry she could hardly stand it. The nurses gave her some swabs to moisten her mouth, but it wasn't much help, and the morphine also caused her to be unable to urinate on her own, so they re-inserted the catheter.

The next day Mariah had two visitors—Dar and Sara. With a concerned look, Sara said, "We got worried when you didn't come home on Friday night. With all the strangeness going on with the shooting, we thought something bad might have happened to you."

"Shooting? I think the nurse mentioned that."

"Yes," replied Sara. "It was over on Murfreesboro Road. Just an altercation that turned into a rampage."

"We called the police station," said Dar, "but they didn't know of anyone by your name. We called the hospital, but they didn't have any information for us, either."

"Boy, you look pretty beat up," blurted Sara. "What happened?"

"I wish you could tell me. I was walking to my car, and someone hit me from behind and I fell forward. That's the last thing I remember."

"I noticed a blood stain on the sidewalk near the parking garage," Sara said softly. "It must be yours."

They were all silent for a moment. Then Mariah asked, "Sombra?"

Dar responded, "I used the key you gave me for emergencies and checked on Sombra to make sure he had food, water, and clean litter.

"Thank you."

"Finally, the hospital got your name and where you worked and called the office," Sara continued. "Is there anything else you need us to check on?"

"No, I don't think so. Oh, wait. What about my car? Is it still in the parking garage?"

"We'll check. Well, we'd better get going. If you'd like us to bring anything next time we come to visit, just call, okay?"

"Sure. Thanks for stopping by."

The next day, word had gotten out and Mariah had a procession of visitors—several other employees from the office and Mr. Hansen, who walked in with a piece of paper flapping in his hand. As he moved closer to her bed, she noticed the familiar smell of his cologne—the subtle, yet woody Givenchy Gentleman. "You know what this is? It's your realtor's license! You are now a real estate agent in my office. Any time you want to sell some real estate, you are free to do so. How are you feeling?"

"Well, I got up today and went to the bathroom with some help from the nurses. It's hard to keep my balance. They say I still have some swelling in my head. I don't think I'll be selling any real estate in the near future."

"I'm so sorry this happened to you," said Mr. Hansen. "And I hope you get better real soon."

"So do I."

He left the room. Mariah was happy to have seen Mr. Hansen but wondered how he even knew where she was. He must have called the office to tell her about the license and they told him.

Once Mariah was able to walk without help, the doctor weaned her off the tubes. She was eating on her own, so she didn't need the glucose solution anymore and she was able to use tablets to control her pain. She was glad they removed the morphine drip, with all its side effects.

Before her discharge, the nurses changed her dressing. The gauze had adhered to the scabs forming on her face and head, so they soaked it with saline before pulling it off. Even so, Mariah felt searing pain each time they took another tug. She tried to be stoic but still cried out. By the time the gauze was off, the scrapes and cuts were bloody and raw. The nurses applied a new bandage, which they assured her wouldn't stick this time.

Dar showed up to take Mariah home, bringing a new change of clothes. Mariah felt weak and vulnerable. She took her clothing into the bathroom for some privacy, but in her weakened state, she had to take rest breaks between putting on each item of clothing. Changing took so long that Dar knocked and asked if she needed help.

On the drive home, Dar told Mariah her car was still in the parking garage. She and Sara didn't have a key, so they weren't able to drive it back. They had talked with Craig about it, and he renewed the parking permit to the end of the month. Knowing she wouldn't be able to drive for a while, Mariah fished out her car keys and gave them to Dar.

At the apartment, Dar had to help Mariah up the stairs. Mariah was so happy to see Sombra, who jumped on the back of the sofa to greet her. She scooped him up and kissed him and kept talking to him. Dar saw she was no longer needed and crept back to the door and let herself out.

Mariah was now aware of the bruising between her legs. Whenever she felt the pain down there, she would start to think about how she had been violated. It hurt to pee, but perhaps that was caused by the catheter. The pain itself wasn't the problem. It was just enough to cause her to think about the attack. Her mind began building images of being raped. She then fantasized about what she wished she had done—how she might have fought off the predator. Kicked him in the groin. Poked his eyes out. Screamed for help. The fact that it was impossible to go back in time added to her feeling of helplessness and her depression grew.

While Mariah was in the hospital, friends could come to see her during visiting hours. The visits had helped her feel loved and supported. Even some folks she didn't realize were her friends stopped in. Now at home, she found herself isolated for hours.

She tired easily and had to take frequent naps. Sometimes she found herself crying for no apparent reason. The most she could do was warm up a can of soup. It was clear she needed to figure out her income. If she couldn't work for a while, how would she be able to make even this month's rent? Homelessness was unimaginable.

It was time to take more pain medications. Mariah brought her water glass to the bathroom sink where she kept the pills in the little cabinet with a hinged mirror. After putting the bottle back, she closed the cabinet and was face-to-face with her image. The left side of her head was still raw with a few stitches showing and bruises ran down to her slightly enlarged chin. Her left eyelid was still so swollen that her eye was only a small slit. The swelling filled in the space between her eyes, so there was no bridge of her nose. Her nose looked bent to the right to accommodate the swelling on the left. Her right eye was wide open and round as if trying to handle the job of both eyes. *Will I ever look normal again?*

Her hair had been shaved on the left. Mariah spent a few minutes playing with the rest of her hair to see if she could disguise any of the injury by changing the part. It didn't work. She decided to tie a scarf around her head as a partial cover whenever she went out.

By the weekend Mariah was more depressed. She had been isolated and lethargic. Her mind was filled with a swirl of thoughts around her situation, the attack, and the meaning it gave her life.

Dar could see that Mariah was struggling with pain and depression. Since she went running every Saturday morning in Percy Warner Park, Dar thought maybe taking Mariah out to the park would lift her spirits. It had been warm for December and Dar felt sure the sun would cheer Mariah up. She reluctantly accepted Dar's invitation, knowing that it might be impossible to enjoy the park, considering how she felt.

The sky was blue, and the sun was bright, so it was a nice drive out to the park, but it was clear across town and the vibration hadn't done Mariah's head any good.

A group of runners had gathered at one end of a grassy area. Dar said, "I'll be running for about an hour, but there's a bench over there if you need to rest." Then she joined the group and jogged off.

Mariah sat on the bench, eyes closed, wishing she could shut out the pain coming from inside her head. The warm sun would have felt good if only a good feeling could come through the curtain of pain. Finally, she opened her eyes and looked around the enormous park. An expanse of lawn met a rock stairway rising up a hill that seemed to have no end. On both sides were paved paths as wide as a road. A lone runner wearing a baseball cap was coming down one of the paths. The runner stopped near the bench and pulled off her cap. Out popped a tousled mass of curly golden hair. The runner shook her head and her hair arranged itself around her shoulders. She smiled at Mariah. "Do you mind if I use this bench for stretching?"

"I guess not," Mariah shrugged. Then, as the runner put one foot on the end of the bench and leaned forward, Mariah put her head and hands on her knees.

The runner asked, "Are you okay?"

"I have a headache; I've had it for weeks, and it's not going away."

"I'm so sorry if I bothered you. My name is Alex. Short for Alexandria." Alex sat down next to Mariah on the bench. "What does your head feel like right this minute?"

"It's throbbing."

"Do you mean the pain comes and goes in a rhythm?"

"Sort of, yeah."

"So, then it's like pain, no pain, and back to pain again, right?"

"Why are you asking me these questions?" Mariah snapped, wishing to be left alone.

Alex smiled. "Because that means you only have half a headache, since between the headaches is no headache. That's good news, isn't it?"

In a droll tone, Mariah replied, "You are beyond Pollyanna."

"Oh, look! Under that bush. See the bunnies?" Alex exclaimed.

Mariah looked and sure enough, wild rabbits were playing under the shrub. She watched for several minutes, smiling at their cuteness.

Then Alex asked, "How does your head feel now—in this moment?"

"Not too bad, right this moment."

Alex stood up. "Well, I have to go now. Try to keep checking in with the present moment. That way you won't miss those times when there's no pain."

Alex waved goodbye with a sweet smile as she jogged away. Mariah was half irritated, and half intrigued by Alex. On one hand, she did feel better after their conversation. But on the other, how intrusive was that? And so unsympathetic.

Still, Mariah found herself checking with her body in the present moment from time to time. Alex was right, often the pain wasn't too bad. Being in the present moment gave Mariah a new perspective.

Finished with her run, Dar strolled over to Mariah. "Ready to go home?"

In the car, Mariah asked, "Have you seen a woman with golden curly hair down to her shoulders or stuffed into a baseball cap?"

"Most people with long hair put it up into a cap in this park. But I might know who you're talking about. There is one woman who runs here almost every day around this time. I don't know her name, but she's super nice—and beautiful."

"That's probably the one," Mariah said. "But why did you say most people wear their hair in a cap?"

"Because of the owl. It attacks people's heads, either because it looks like an animal from above or maybe it wants hair for its nest. Either way, it really hurts when it attacks."

"The woman said her name is Alex, short for Alexandria."

"Yes, I remember now, that's the one. I've seen her many times. Sometimes she joins the group I run with. She always seems so joyful. It's fun to be around her."

"I didn't know how to take her," Mariah mumbled. "She was a little too happy. I didn't like it."

Chapter Seven

Mariah rode with Dar and Sara to the office on Monday. She was hoping to get back to work as she faced impending financial disaster. She went directly to Craig to talk about coming back to work. Once there, she stopped in the ladies' room to try to reposition her headscarf to cover the worst of the scars. Then she walked across the hall to Craig's door and knocked.

"Come on in," responded Craig. "Dar told me you'd be stopping by. What can I do for you?"

"I'm hoping to come back to work," Mariah stammered. "I know someone else probably fixed the filing, but maybe there is still something I can do?"

"We had to hire another person to go ahead on this project. But I'll tell you what. Our Christmas party is this Friday. It's later than we usually do it, and the party arrangements are way behind schedule. We could pay you to stick around this week and help organize the party and be a host. That will get you to the end of the month at least."

Mariah looked away and then said quietly, "Thanks. Who should I talk to?"

"Check with Hannah. I think she's working on it and getting overwhelmed."

Mariah left Craig's office and headed straight across the hall to the ladies' room trying to hide the tears welling in her eyes. *The last paycheck in December will be tiny. I don't even know if I can pay another month's rent. It would be hard to get another job looking like this, and besides, this time of year there are probably not many opportunities available.* She stayed in the restroom until she put her emotions in check, then headed to the front desk to talk to Hannah.

Hannah welcomed Mariah cheerfully. "I'm so happy Craig got me some help," she chirped. "Normally we do the Christmas party a week earlier, but I just didn't get started until too late, so we postponed it until this week. I hope it's not too late to get all the usual guests."

"Who gets invited?"

"Every year all the closing attorneys invite the realtors they work with to a big Christmas party. It's a huge deal. The realtors spend most of December going from one party to another. We have wine and lavish spreads of party food."

"Wow. What would you like me to do?"

Hannah was busy answering the phone, so she scrawled a note to Mariah to be in the conference room where the party committee would be meeting at one o'clock.

Mariah wandered down the hall to hang out with Sara just to watch her work. Sara smiled but let Mariah know she was busy and couldn't be distracted. She flew through the files, checking numbers and closing instructions. She seemed to immediately catch any possible errors.

"There," Sara said, closing and putting away the files. "That's all I have for the rest of the week. It gets slower and slower toward Christmas time. I'd offer to go to lunch with you, but I already have a date. That cute attorney. I thought he was single, but it turns out he has a steady girlfriend. He must be getting a wandering eye, though, since he asked me to lunch today." With that, Sara squirmed in the way she always did when thinking about men.

Mariah went down to the coffee shop, bought a sandwich, and took it up to eat in the conference room before the meeting started. The committee worked on decor and food arrangements. They planned for five stations, each with a different kind of food—meat and cheese plates, salads, little sandwiches, hot appetizers, and desserts. The food would be catered but by different caterers. Mariah's assignment was to order the plates, utensils, wine glasses, and table-cloths, and Hannah suggested three potential party rental places she could check with. Hannah was working on the decorations and the others split up the food assignments.

The owner of the first place Mariah called laughed when she made her request. "Sorry, we booked up all our supplies long ago." The next call was a bit more congenial, but they could not come up with the number of items she required. The third company agreed to supply the party, but the supplies would not be ready until Friday morning just before the event started. It was nerve-wracking, but with no alternative, Mariah booked it. She spent the rest of the afternoon helping Hannah with decorations.

On the way home, Mariah told Dar and Sara the bad news about her job.

"It's common for real estate work to dry up around the holidays," said Sara. "But it'll likely pick up gradually at the beginning of the year." That's when Mariah confided she would have to put in her last month's notice on the apartment because she wouldn't be able to afford it beyond that.

"Well, what are you going to do?" asked Dar.

Mariah wailed, "I don't know!"

Sara wrinkled her nose. "Please don't tell me you are just going to manifest again."

"Why not?" Mariah said, regaining her footing.

"Okay, here's the deal, Mariah. How did you manifest getting attacked? Did you manifest being in the hospital for a week?"

Dar shouted, "Sara, lay off! She didn't choose to be attacked. Mariah, I'm sorry. We'll be here to help you with whatever you need."

Sara cut in, "I didn't mean it as a criticism of you, Mariah. I just don't believe in the woo-woo stuff, and I feel kind of protective of you."

"I'm not sure I believe in the woo-woo stuff anymore, either. I thought I could manage my life to be whatever I wanted and here's what I got instead. The universe is not my friend, apparently. And now I don't know what to do."

"Maybe you shouldn't try to manage life," said Sara. "It's not like you can boss 'The Universe' around, you know."

Mariah spent Thursday helping other members of the committee prepare for the party. Her part wouldn't happen until late Friday morning. That's when she would need everyone to frantically help put it all together.

Friday was a flurry of activity. Finally, the tablecloths, dishes, and glasses arrived. The tablecloths needed some ironing. No one had an iron, so they tried to hide the wrinkles under food plates. Mariah unpacked and laid out the glasses. By mid-afternoon, people began filing in. Mariah wasn't tied to a station, so she was supposed to wander around greeting the guests and fetching things for the team. It made her uncomfortable to be seen in this role, with her scabby face, but gradually she lost her self-consciousness. An hour later, she spotted Mr. Hansen.

"Hi, Mariah. How are you doing?"

"Well, I'm getting better, Mr. Hansen."

"I'm glad to hear it, but please call me Dick."

"Okay, Dick. I'll have to get used to it, though."

"You're part of my office now, you know? Since I hold your realtor's license, it would be a good idea to come to my office and get to know the rest of the family. When do you think you can do that?"

Mariah thought for a moment. "Well, I think I'll be free all of next week."

"Most of the folks at the office will be taking the bridge week off, but I would like to talk with you. Why don't you stop by around the first of the year?"

"I'll do that," said Mariah as she walked away to greet some more guests.

Christmas was the saddest day Mariah could ever remember. She had always loved the scents of fir boughs, cinnamon, and chocolate mint. Longing for the time when the smells, colors, and sounds of Christmas meant happiness to her, it all seemed flat. As an only child, Mariah always felt she and her parents were a tight threesome. They spent the whole day together, opening presents, drinking hot chocolate and mulled cider, and putting together a new jigsaw puzzle. Now the world appeared to be falling apart around her and loneliness loomed large. Her parents were still unreachable. She hadn't left a phone number or address for her old friends when she moved. She also didn't feel like calling them because the news of her life seemed so sad, and she didn't think of them as friends anyway. For them to accept her boyfriend of four years and Sandra, her best friend, as a couple still seemed like a slap in the face. Sara and Dar had family of their own to spend the weekend with and that left Mariah alone with way too much thinking time. She considered putting in her notice on the apartment. The last month's payment would be covered by the deposit, but to get another place, she'd probably need to put down a first, last, and cleaning deposit. She would only have one month to get that.

Mariah tried not to think about it, but she couldn't remember when she had her last period. It might have been at the beginning of this month. It had never occurred to her to be charting those things. She wasn't sure at what point a pregnancy test would show accurate results. Next week she resolved to buy a home test. In the meantime, there was nothing to do but worry. The specter of pregnancy made her nauseous, but she couldn't block it from her mind.

Sunday was cold and crisp but with a clear sky. Mariah thought a walk in that lovely park would pick up her spirits. She drove across town and found the park empty, as far as she could tell. She thought she might explore one of the meandering paths. As she started walking, choosing the shortest loop, she wondered if the scarf she had on was enough to keep the owl away. Halfway along the loop, she was huffing and out of breath. It must have been a common place for people to run out of steam because there was a bench carved out of a big log right in front of her. She sat, agonizing over all the bad things that were happening to her. Deep in thought, she didn't even notice when Alexandria walked up.

"Hi!"

Startled, Mariah asked, "Where did you come from, Alex?"

"I was just taking my cool-down walk. How are you doing? Did the headache go away?"

"Almost," sighed Mariah. "But everything else is worse."

"What are you talking about?" Alex was bent over in a hamstring stretch. "Here we are on a beautiful, crisp, sunny day in the most wonderful park ever. What's terrible about that?"

"You're right, this is a wonderful park. That's why I came here—to try to cheer up."

"Doesn't look like you are succeeding. What's bothering you?"

"My whole life is just falling apart. It feels like it is sucking me down into a quicksand of depression." Mariah turned toward Alex and pulled off her scarf. "Look at my face! I've lost my job and won't be able to pay the rent after next month."

Alex straightened up and started stretching side to side. "Actually, I think your face looks a whole lot better than it did last time I saw you. And how do you know you won't be able to pay the rent after next month? Can you see that far in the future?"

"Not really, but I also can't see how I am going to get a job and money, either."

"Maybe you just need to trust The Universe," said Alex, "When you don't have a clear idea of what to do next, it's often helpful to relax and be open. Perhaps life needs time to clear a path for you. And that time could be put to good use clearing your preconceived notions about what's possible and what's not."

Mariah shuffled back to her car, angrily wondering how she could ever trust a universe that let her get attacked and raped. And she was mad at Alex for being so cheerful about everything.

The day after New Year brought some nasty weather. The wind blew. It rained. It snowed, too, but didn't stick. For a while, a layer of cold wet slush coated the walkways. Mariah stayed indoors until late in the afternoon when she realized she would have to go grocery shopping. Thinking about conserving her dwindling funds, she picked up only the minimum supplies for the week. Walking through the store, she noticed out of the corner of her eye some people staring at her face. She changed direction, so the scarred side was next to the shelves. She had never felt so bad about her appearance. Seeing a sign pointing to the restroom, she entered, locked herself into a stall, and let herself cry. It wasn't just about her face. It was everything. She felt weak and unable to manage her life anymore. Grief over all she had lost was taking control.

Chapter Eight

Mariah picked up the ringing phone.

"Hey, it's Martha from Jackson & Veronne. I've got your December check ready"

"Thanks, I'll come right over."

On the way to the office, Mariah decided to stop at the library. Maybe she could find a job to apply for while she was there. Parking in the same garage she'd used the night she was attacked; she felt a wave of apprehension. Inside the library, she grabbed a copy of *The Tennessean* and positioned herself in her favorite comfy chair. She started reading the job classifieds. It made her drowsy and soon enough, she fell into a sound sleep.

"Scuse me, are you alright?"

Surprised, Mariah looked up to see an overweight woman wearing a name tag. "I'm fine. Reading always puts me to sleep." She got up and put the newspaper away. In front of the newspaper stacks, she realized she could look for a report of her attack. The paper from the morning after the attack was rumpled and worn as if it had been read by more people than the other days' papers. The front page had more than one article about a shooting on Murfreesboro Road. She followed the pages deeper into the paper but found nothing related to her.

Sighing, she returned to her original purpose. Perhaps the business books would have information on companies she could apply to. She pulled out a large business directory and stared at it for almost a half hour before putting it back without having made any notes at all.

It was getting late in the afternoon, and she still hadn't picked up her check. She may have been dreading seeing the amount, but she finally pushed herself to cross the street and get it. Of course, several people in the office stopped to say hello and ask her what she was up to now. By the time she reached the business office, Martha was just leaving. Martha circled back to grab Mariah's check and handed it to her.

It was already getting dark as she walked a few blocks to her car. The streetlight was still flickering. As Mariah started to pass it, she began to tremble. A cold sweat beaded up on her forehead, stinging the few raw places left after the scabs came off. As the blood left her head, she felt herself sinking to the ground. She crawled forward until she was back on her feet. Quickly entering the garage, she took the elevator to her floor. Once in her car, she began to shake all over. She sat there with the doors locked until the shaking stopped, then drove straight home.

All Mariah wanted to do was sleep. She skipped supper and snuggled into bed with Sombra. When she next opened her eyes, light was slanting through the window. Sombra was starving. Usually a quiet cat, he meowed loudly until Mariah opened the can and served its fishy-smelling contents, making her feel queasy.

Mariah sat sipping coffee in the only dining chair with an unbroken seat and stared at an uneaten sliced banana over a bowl of oatmeal. She'd calculated that her period was overdue. It wasn't easy to keep track of the days. She hadn't told anyone about being raped and was hoping she wouldn't have to. How many days did she have to wait for a pregnancy test? She could call somewhere to find out. Maybe the health department. They probably do some pregnancy screening, as well as other kinds ... Mariah froze. STD screening! What if the rapist had a sexually transmitted disease? With AIDS constantly in the news, the possibility of contracting it could be life-threatening if not extremely embarrassing. Although she managed to stay upright, the cold, clammy, I'm-about-to-faint feeling was more than she could stand. She grabbed the blanket off her bed and wrapped herself in it. She'd better go to the health department next morning. The evening was cold. The temperature had dropped a good ten degrees—almost to freezing. Mariah stayed alone in her apartment stewing over her pending medical tests.

Snowflakes tickled her bedroom window when she woke. She pulled the covers all the way over her head and rolled over on her side. Sombra found the tunnel inviting and curled up next to her under the covers. Over the rest of the day, the snow kept coming down until almost six inches piled up on steps and railings. About three inches covered the streets and sidewalks. It was no time to be going out and neither was the next day.

Mariah again sat at her dining table drinking coffee and this time actually eating the oatmeal she made. Finally, after three days of snow and then nasty slush, the temperature rose, and the rain finished melting away the last of it.

The metro public health department was on the west side of town. Mariah headed there first thing. She was nervous about being seen in this environment, though an unemployed person could get tested for a low fee. She tentatively walked up to the big glass doors and looked around for the right department. The woman at the front desk looked like she was filing her nails and didn't give Mariah eye contact. Finally, Mariah walked up to her and asked where she should go for STD and pregnancy testing. The woman directed her down the hallway to another desk.

"Is this the right place for STD testing?"

"It depends," said a frail-looking woman with stringy dark brown hair. Are you registered with us?"

"No," said Mariah. "I want to apply for assistance. I am unemployed."

The stringy-haired woman handed her a clipboard with five forms to fill out. *This is going to take all day.* But the paperwork went quickly. She brought it to another woman, who took the forms and told her to wait until she was called. By the time Mariah returned to her chair, it had already been taken. For a while she stood, surveying the room. She wanted to disappear. Eventually, someone's name was called, and Mariah took his chair. Most of the people were dressed in old clothes in some stage of disrepair. They sat forward with their arms on their thighs and their heads down, looking at the floor. Mariah began to imagine what kind of trouble each of them had gotten into. Some had bruises. Others looked on the verge of tears. Mariah hated this place. She didn't feel that she belonged with these people.

It took an hour and a half before she was finally called into an exam room. The nurse asked her all kinds of questions. Who had she had sex with? How many people? These questions felt maddeningly invasive. In addition to the disease testing, the nurse gave Mariah a pregnancy test. It was negative. The nurse warned her, though, that it might be too early to get a good result.

By the time Mariah left the health department, "bad mood" would have been an understatement. She drove toward Dick Hansen Realty since she'd said she would visit sometime, and it was not far. She pulled into the small parking lot but just sat in her car. She couldn't see Mr. Hansen in this state of mind.

She was near her favorite park, so she drove there. Even though it was not raining, the snow melt had kept the ground saturated with water, so no one could venture off the asphalt pathway. Mariah found a bench close to the path. The park's beauty was lost on her as she sat absorbed in her anger and depression. Looking straight ahead without moving her eyes or her body, she rehashed all the injustices she had endured. Mariah was no longer friends with The Universe.

"Hi, there!"

With a start, Mariah looked up to see Alex.

"Hi to you, too. I don't feel like talking today."

"Well, we all have our ups and downs sometimes, I guess. When you do feel like talking, I'm always here for you."

Mariah folded her arms and turned away from Alex. "You wouldn't have any idea what I'm going through. I heard you are rich and live in a mansion somewhere around here."

"So what? Didn't you ever hear that money doesn't buy happiness?"

"You always seem way too happy, to me. I have deeper problems than you could even imagine."

"Do you mind if I sit here?" asked Alex.

"Yes, I do mind. I told you I don't feel like talking."

"That's okay, I'll do the talking and you can sit there in silence if that's what you want." After a moment or so of Mariah's silence, Alex sat down. "I wasn't always so cheerful. It took me a long time to find happiness inside me. There was a time when I wanted to commit suicide."

"Why?"

"It's a long story. My husband and I met in college. He wanted to be in the music business and finally got a gig as a roadie in a band that did pretty well. I quit college and followed him on the road. He worked hard and eventually became the band's sound engineer. I didn't see much of him, even though we were traveling together. When he wasn't around, some of the men were threatening. I never felt safe. I didn't seem to have any control over my life. I just followed along.

Then my husband was able to move to Nashville and work at a record label. He signed a couple of popular groups and started making a lot of money. Eventually, we moved to our house here in Belle Meade. That's when I started getting depressed. It seemed like my husband didn't want me to do anything but be beautiful and by his side when he went to parties and award banquets."

"You were arm candy."

"That's right, arm candy. He didn't want me to work. I didn't even do housework because he had hired a maid. It seemed like everything for him was about showing off his success—including me. I sat around and ate snacks. Pretty soon I was getting fat. I lost my self-confidence. My husband started leaving hints that he was dissatisfied with me, and I thought he might be having an affair. That's when I was at my lowest. I began planning my suicide."

"How did you pull out of it? I mean what did you do about it?"

"I went to a bookstore and started reading everything I could on self-improvement. Since I had unlimited time on my hands, I went every day. Then I started running, which improved my outlook a lot. The self-improvement books led me to study spirituality. And finally, I also started doing volunteer work to help others. I think that's an important part of getting out of a funk or away from self-sabotage."

"What kind of volunteer work do you do?"

"I volunteer at the hospital. I just go around to the rooms and ask people if they want someone to visit with. You know, some of those patients are pretty lonely up there. And if the patient doesn't respond at all, sometimes I just sing to them."

"Oh wait! Was that you? When I was in the hospital someone came in and sang to me. I thought it was an angel!"

"Thank you. I'm sure it was me. I don't know of anyone else who sings up there. So anyway, I know my story probably doesn't seem so bad to you. It just shows that anyone can get depressed by what they think about their situation, whether it is bad or not."

"Well, my story really is bad. And it's not just what I'm thinking about it."

Alex stood up. "I know you have the strength to get through whatever it is. And I can tell you from experience that nothing can stop you from being happy, no matter what it is. Bye now!" Mariah had her doubts about getting through it, but Alex's story gave her some credibility.

Mariah could almost look at it as an inspiration. And thinking about the time Alex sang to her in the hospital room gave her goosebumps.

Chapter Nine

It was the weekend and Mariah was beginning to feel the need for some social interaction. She walked over to Dar's apartment and knocked on the door.

"Oh, hi," said Dar. "How are you doing?"

"Do you have time to chat a bit?" asked Mariah.

"Well, I'm studying for exams right now, but we could chat for a few minutes. What's on your mind?"

"I just wanted to catch up. I don't see you guys much anymore. In fact, I haven't seen Sara for days."

"Sara is seeing Kyle now and doesn't even come home at night. Want to sit down? Can I get you some coffee or tea?"

"Tea, please."

Mariah sat on a stool at the kitchen counter, and Dar stood across from her. "Kyle? Isn't that the new attorney? Do you think she's staying over at his house?"

"Most likely."

"Is the work picking up at Jackson & Veronne?"

Dar set the teacup in front of Mariah. "Do you want sugar or anything? It's still slow at work."

"No, thank you. I haven't found a job yet and my rent runs out in a little over a week. I'll be out of money and homeless. I never thought I would be in this position."

"What kind of work have you been looking for?"

"Nothing! I have had all these worries and pain and depression. And the snow days didn't help, either."

"I don't know of any job openings. Why don't you check with some of your other connections? Like . . . what about the real estate instructor? He seems to like you."

"You're right. He asked me to stop by his office this month and I haven't yet. I'm not sure it would do me any good. Real estate agents work on commission, and I can't afford that."

"Don't forget the power of connections. He works with a lot of people, so he might be able to refer you to someone else."

"Oh, yeah, I didn't think about it that way. I'll go see him first thing on Monday. Thanks for the suggestion."

Mariah's spirits were lifted as she went back to her apartment. She started making plans for what she would say to Mr. Hansen when she saw him. And with her lifted spirits, she wondered if she could talk about her situation to Alexandria. Mariah hadn't been very receptive to her the last few times, but she was beginning to want Alex's positive outlook.

Sunday afternoon was sunny and just under sixty degrees. This time Mariah headed to Percy Warner Park actually hoping to find Alex. The lot was almost full, and people were everywhere. Families were spreading blankets on the ground for a picnic. Others were playing games. As Mariah wound her way through the crowd, her eyes scanned the distance for a glimpse of Alex. She was beginning to think it was a lost cause when she saw someone lean against a bench just like Alex. Mariah walked closer. Sure enough.

Mariah called out, "Hello."

"What a surprise!" chirped Alex. "What brings you here today?"

"I was actually looking for you. You always seem so cheerful and happy when I see you, and now that I know what you've been through, I'd like to learn more about how I can get some happiness, too."

"Sure, I'd be delighted to talk with you some more. I was just stretching to get ready for a run, but I can run later."

"I don't even know where to start," said Mariah.

"Well, when were you happy, and how did you lose your happiness?"

"I was pretty happy when I moved here last summer. I got a job right away and a place to live, thanks to a couple of new friends I made. I thought I was working with The Universe to manifest my dream, but then I was attacked and ended up in the hospital. My job was given to another person and nothing new has come up. I put in the last month's notice for my apartment because I don't have enough money for the rent. I have to move out in just a little over a week, and then I'll be homeless—unless I have a miracle."

Alex was quiet for a moment. "I've always noticed that when my prayers are finally answered, I never saw it coming. One day things look bleak and suddenly it all turns around. It's like The Universe is working out the details in the background until the right moment. The key to being happy in a bleak situation is to relax. You can do more damage by being anxious than relaxed."

"I think that's easier said than done." Mariah was twisting around on the bench trying to find a comfortable position. "And I don't trust the universe anymore."

"That's when you need to manage your thinking."

Mariah furrowed her brow. "How on earth can I manage my thinking and what does that have to do with everything I've been through?"

"Well, the way I look at it, it's not about what happened, but what you *think* about what happened. You have free will over how you react to things. First, stop judging them as good or bad. I use gratitude for that. And I welcome everything that happens as an opportunity."

Mariah rolled her eyes and turned away. She was starting to feel queasy over all this positivity. "Maybe I'm just not ready to go that far," she said.

"Start by being specific. Instead of thinking about 'all that I've been through,' think about one issue at a time. What is the most pressing thing for you right now?"

"Getting a job and finding a place to live—in that order, I guess."

"See? You've already named two opportunities! Be grateful for that sense of direction and ask The Universe to show you what to do next to achieve it. And relax."

"Thanks, Alex. I'll let you get that run in. I do feel a little more positive about things now. That's something to think about, the idea that getting a job and finding a home are opportunities, not problems."

"Good! And find me again to tell me how it worked out." Alex trotted off, calling bye-bye over her shoulder.

Monday morning Mariah was eager to touch base with Dick Hansen. She took a deep breath and dialed his number.

"Hello, Mr. . . . uh, Dick? This is Mariah. I could come out to your office today if you still want me to. What time would work best for you?"

"Can you leave now? How long will it take you to get here? We're on Charlotte Pike. You have my card, right?"

"Yes, I can be there in thirty minutes. See you soon."

The office was clear across Nashville from Mariah's apartment. On the way, she tried Alex's idea and thought about being grateful for the appointment, but she wondered why on earth Dick was so eager to meet her.

Dick was waiting when Mariah arrived. The realty office consisted of a small reception area with two rooms (former bedrooms), a kitchen, and a bathroom, all painted a dull beige. One of the bedrooms had five desks arranged haphazardly. The other bedroom was smaller with only one large desk and bookshelves. That was Dick's office, but he sat Mariah down at the reception desk in what had been a living room and pulled up a nearby chair.

"I was impressed with you in the classes I taught. You took in the information so calmly and didn't get flustered like the others in the class. That's why I was hoping you would take the test and get your license with me. You seem solid and dependable, and that's a good trait in real estate. Many people think they can get by with a flashy 'out-there' personality. That works in the beginning, but it wears thin after a while."

"Well, I hope you didn't ask me to come here to sell real estate in the office," said Mariah. "That would be impossible for me right now. I'm almost out of money. I'm going to have to find a paying job right away." Tears began welling up in Mariah's lower eyelids. "I put in my one-month notice at the apartment, and I have no idea if I can even find a cheaper place to rent."

"I see," said Dick. "I've been thinking about doing some hiring for this year. We laid off our receptionist a few months ago when there was not much for her to do. I also had a rental manager who took care of ten rental properties I own. She lived in one of the rental houses, but she moved away at the end of November. Would you consider taking her place and also doing reception work?"

Mariah's breath caught. *Could Alex be right?*

"What would that entail?" she asked.

"The rental properties don't need much. You would take the renter's calls if there was a problem at one of the houses—leaks, that sort of thing. You'll have a list of contractors you can call once you know what the problem is and what's needed. You collect the rent and keep track of the checks coming in, as well as the expenses. The house is a small two-bedroom with a studio behind it. The guy who lives in the studio has reduced rent because he takes care of the landscape maintenance. I've heard he's unemployed right now, so you can probably get him to help with yard maintenance of the other properties, too.

"My original reason for wanting you in the office is that a few of our newer realtors are insecure about financing. As you know, the interest rates are so high right now that many buyers want to explore creative types of mortgages. You picked that up so quickly in class, it would be a great asset here if you would be available to help them out. To be honest, I need someone like you. I'm not in the office enough to help them that much."

Puzzled, Mariah asked, "So, what are you offering, exactly?"

"I could pay you to work in the office. You would answer the phone and give any new clients or walk-ins to one of the agents. Choose whoever is a good match or whoever happens to be there. And you could live in the house rent-free for taking care of all the other rentals."

"How soon would you want me to start?"

"As soon as possible. As I said, I can't be here in the office very much, and we need someone to answer the phone at the very least. We can't pay much more than minimum wage, but you would have low expenses because of free rent. What do you say?"

After a long pause, Mariah said, "I have to move out of my apartment next week. Can I start immediately?"

Dick smiled broadly. "I was hoping you'd say that."

They shook hands and Dick gave her an office key and his home phone number. "Come in tomorrow morning, and I'll give you more instructions and take you over to see the rental house."

In the morning, Mariah called Dick. He seemed vague about the time he could meet. He finally asked her to come to the office around ten and, if there was no one there, to let herself in with the key and call to see if he could come.

Mariah agreed. She began packing to move before leaving her apartment at nine-thirty. When she got to the office, the door was unlocked, and two agents were already at their desks. She went to the front desk phone and called Dick. He said he still couldn't come in yet and asked her to wait. He would call her when he was able to get away.

Meanwhile, Mariah introduced herself to the other agents. She recognized one of them from her class, although they had not spoken to each other before. Her name was Clara. She had long straight hair parted in the middle with bangs. Her thick-rimmed glasses reminded Mariah more of a librarian than a real estate agent. The other, Mark, was an older gentleman who seemed like he had been with the brokerage for a long time. His hair was thinning on top and had been dyed with a men's hair product that looked light brown most of the time, but when the sun shone across his head, it was a pinkish lavender. She told them she would be working there as a receptionist.

Clara said, "I remember you from the class because you were so smart, and Mr. Hansen seemed particularly fond of you."

"Well, I'm glad for the job," said Mariah. "The timing is right. Why does Dick have so much trouble coming into the office?"

Mark replied, "He takes care of his sick wife."

Mariah was relieved to hear that Dick had a wife. She was worried that maybe Dick had an ulterior motive for giving her a job and a house to live in. She didn't want to feel as if she owed him something for bailing her out of her situation.

Dick finally called in and Mariah answered, "Hansen Realty, Mariah speaking."

"Nice!" said Dick. "I'll be there in ten minutes."

He arrived in only eight, grabbed the keys to the rental house and the two of them caravanned to the rental even though it was only about four blocks away. Mariah commented that she would be walking to work. And what a nice thing, not having to drive and pay for parking.

The house needed updating like the apartment she was leaving. A beige counter divided the kitchen from the combined dining and living room. The tile bathroom offered a full tub with a shower. The two bedrooms were very small with minuscule closets. The flower beds around the whole house looked like one of those English cottage yards except with a plain brown and beige box of a house.

"Okay, this will be fine. I'll try to get a truck to move this weekend. In the meantime, do you want me to start working regular hours in the office?"

"Why don't you come in about ten and leave at four? And if you wouldn't mind, have the agents call you if they need any help with contracts. Okay?"

"All right."

Dick abruptly handed Mariah the house keys and left.

Chapter Ten

Mariah called to see if Dar could offer any help with moving. Dar was happy to hear that she had found a job and a house to live in but couldn't take time away from her exams to help. Sara was out of town, and no one knew when she'd be back. Remembering the yard sale where she'd gotten her furniture, Mariah dug up the church's phone number and asked if they knew anyone who could help carry furniture down her apartment stairs into a small van. She could pay them. The signature fifteen-minute wait yielded the names of two possible helpers, one of whom she recognized. Ken was the man who had helped get the furniture from the church. That meant he had a truck, too. Mariah called him right away.

"Hello, Ken? This is Mariah McKenzie. A few months ago, you delivered some furniture from the church yard sale. Do you remember?"

"Well heck, yeah, I do remember," said Ken. "What kin I do for ya?"

"I'm moving again and I need help. Could you do it this Saturday? I'll pay you."

"Gosh, Mariah, I don't know. I think I have to do a yard cleanup this Saturday—that's what I do mostly. I know another guy. I can send him to you. Give me yer number and I'll have him call."

"Thank you so much. Do you know how much he charges?"

"I don't know. Might not charge anything if he's not busy, pretty girl like you. . . ."

"I'll definitely pay him. Does he have a truck?"

"You bet he does. A fine truck."

Mariah thanked Ken and hung up the phone. She wondered if the scars on her head made her ugly enough to keep the friend at a distance.

About an hour after she called Ken, the phone rang. It was Jason, Ken's friend. Jason said he would come on Saturday morning around ten, and they agreed on a price.

On Thursday, Mariah showed up at the real estate office at the time Dick had designated. A few agents whom she hadn't met yet sat at their desks: Harry, a small, slender young man, and Gretchen, in her thirties. According to Mark, there was one other agent, Marla, who'd been with the company forever, but she would only come into the office when she had a hot deal. She wouldn't give anyone in the office the time of day.

Dick must have already told the office about Mariah because Harry, Clara, and Gretchen all assured her they would have her check the numbers before they drew up a contract. Also, they expressed gratitude that she would be there to help with financing decisions for their clients.

In the middle of the afternoon, Mariah heard a shriek coming from the room with five desks, followed by sobs. When she went to check, Gretchen was crying hard, and the others were all trying to comfort her.

"What happened?" asked Mariah.

Everyone turned to Gretchen, who seemed inconsolable.

Through sobs, she said, "My two high schoolers were scrapbooking on the couch and got into a fight. One of the children stabbed the scissors into the leather couch. I feel like never going home because I can't stand the idea of seeing it." *Jeez, that sofa must mean a lot to her.*

Later that day, a new client called in about an ad. Mariah knew she couldn't give the call to Gretchen, who was still in a tizzy. It was a young woman, and Mariah had to decide between Harry and Clara. She chose Clara, who seemed very excited to be given the call. The caller told Clara she would be right over. Clara paced around the office waiting for the client, but finally gave up around four o'clock and went home. Mariah wondered why the woman hadn't come in.

Dick called. "Mariah, how did the day go?"

"It was pretty crazy. Gretchen got all upset over something her kids had done. I guess they stabbed her leather couch or something, but she cried most of the day and refused to go home because she didn't want to see it. And Harry was fawning all over her trying to console her. Then someone called about a house, so I gave the call to Clara. She talked to them awhile, but she had to keep putting her hand over the receiver to block the noise of Gretchen's crying. The caller never showed up. I don't know if that had anything to do with the crying, but I could tell Clara was annoyed."

"Clara is still pretty new here. When you take a call, try to get as much information as possible. Get a call-back number if you can. You can ask if they own a home they would need to sell, or if they are renters—things like that.

Maybe Clara was nervous. You could give her a pep talk about qualifying the clients like I taught in class."

"I'm not sure what I would say. I remember what you taught us, but I don't even have as much real estate experience as Clara."

"I do need you to maintain a professional atmosphere in the office. We can't have Gretchen ruining business."

"I don't know what I can do about it. I don't feel I have the authority to boss her around."

"Well, do your best with that. I have to go now."

The next day Gretchen was still in a crying mood and only Harry was willing to entertain her. Clara had decided to do some phone cold calling and confided that she wished Gretchen would leave so her calls would not have wailing in the background. When Harry and Gretchen left for lunch, Clara got it going.

Once Clara gave herself a break, Mariah said, "I admire you for making those calls. Some people would find themselves too shy to do something like that." Mariah was thinking of herself.

"I look at it as a way to help people. I have services to offer and if they need those services, they'd be thrilled to hear from me. If they aren't—no big deal. I go on to the next call."

Wow, thought Mariah, that's a great attitude. She asked Clara about the woman who didn't show up yesterday and Clara explained it probably was a "lookie-loo," who wasn't ready to buy a house and just wanted to dream. Clara didn't need a pep talk. By the evening, she had made two appointments—one for her to see a potential listing and another to show homes to a qualified buyer. She was feeling pretty proud of herself.

Mariah was worried about Jason, after what Ken had said about her looks. To feel safe, she decided to go see the man who lived in the little cottage behind her new house. Even if he didn't offer to help her move, at least he might be willing to be visible in the yard so that Jason knew he would not be able to catch her alone.

Mariah knocked on the cottage door. A young man opened it, bare-chested and smelling like clean sweat. He had tan skin, straight dark hair, and deep brown eyes.

"Hi, my name is Mariah. I'm moving into the house here."

"I'm Arthur. Is there anything you need?"

"I was just hoping you would be around, maybe just out here in the yard. I don't know the man who is helping me move and I want to be safe. I think if he saw you were around, he wouldn't try to do anything other than move furniture and boxes. You know what I mean?"

"I'll be here in the yard weeding," he said.

Jason showed up precisely at ten o'clock, as agreed. It wasn't a big job—just carrying the furniture down the apartment stairs, which was easy with Mariah holding one end and Jason taking the other. Mariah shoved her few boxes in the spaces between the furniture to keep them from shifting in Jason's pickup. No reason to worry about damaging that furniture, it was already old and dinged up. Unloading proceeded uneventfully.

Mariah spent the rest of the day setting up her new home, unpacking boxes, and making the bed. Sombra seemed especially lost, wandering around the house trying to get used to things. By nighttime, she was able to relax, and they both slept soundly.

Sunday morning, the one thing Mariah wanted was to go to the park, which was now much closer to her home. Her goal was to visit the park every day, if possible, and get fit until she could walk or run on the trails. When she arrived, the park was full of people. She started hiking up the shortest route along with several other groups. Again, she was winded by the time she got to the bench. While she rested, her thoughts swirled. So many things were happening. She was relieved to have a house to live in and a job, but on the other hand, puzzled about Dick Hansen's motive. Was he being overly generous to offer the house and the job? What does he want in return? And did he want her to manage the office? Will he ever show up and be the boss? It felt like he was expecting a lot of her. With *no experience* selling real estate!

Mariah walked down the hill to her car. She was refreshed—even invigorated. It reinforced her resolve to do this every day.

She looked around for Alex but didn't see her.

Later, Mariah returned to her old apartment to check for any forgotten things and to clean. Sara and Dar knocked on the door, bearing a bottle of wine and some plastic glasses. "We wanted to see you off," said Sara.

"Sara, you're back!"

"Well, not for long. I'm leaving again Monday, and I'll probably be on the road for quite a while."

"What?" asked Mariah. "What are you talking about?"

"I met a guy," Sara said while opening the wine and pouring it into glasses. "He's taking me places—even out of the country—and he has hooked me up with a travel agency where I can take tours and eventually lead them."

"You mean you're leaving Jackson & Verrone? Why? You're so smart, Sara. Why would you leave a job, where your brain is useful, to run around for a travel company? Aren't you wasting your intelligence?"

"Despite working for a law firm, I never wanted to be a real estate attorney. That's why I didn't go to law school."

"Then what made you want to work there in the first place?"

"I watched a lot of TV shows about law firms and I thought the guys were really cute. I wanted to be in a place where there were good-looking men, but it turns out attorneys are not all that hunky after all."

"Oh, lord," sighed Mariah.

Dar sat quietly on the floor.

"Don't judge me for what I want to do," said Sara. "I feel no responsibility whatsoever to use my brain. I like being with men. And whenever being with one man is no longer exciting, I just move on to the next. I don't see anything wrong with doing what I love to do, and travel seems like a great fit for me. We all need to find what we love—and do it."

Mariah was silent for several minutes and then murmured, "I'm not sure I've found what I love. I wonder if it'll ever happen for me. And I may as well forget about men."

"Why do you say that?" asked Sara.

"Look at me! I'm damaged goods. I have a disfigured face. I haven't had much luck with men anyway. And I don't think of my work as being something to love, either."

"Don't be a sad sack, Mariah," Sara scolded.

Mariah looked at Sara. "You know, maybe I'm just jealous of you. Here you are with a genius brain and have men flocking all around you. I'm not sure I'll ever find love."

"Have you even tried? I never even saw you flirt with anyone in the office. You need to at least put some effort into dating.

Mariah tipped her head back. "It's not that I wasn't willing. It seemed to me that like all the best men were already married and the rest were unreliable playboys. I'm not looking for sexual excitement—more like a long-term partner. I did think Craig was kind of cute, but I don't believe inter-office relationships are appropriate."

Sara and Dar looked at each other with a knowing smile. "You would have been disappointed if you tried," said Sara. "He has a steady boyfriend."

"Oh," Mariah sighed, "I don't know if the right man for me even exists. They're either already taken or the wrong type."

The next morning when it was time to go to work, Mariah decided to take the alley behind the house and see if it would lead to the office because it's more fun to look in all the neighbors' backyards. The gate was padlocked. She tried the small key Dick had given her with the house key and sure enough, it worked. She noticed more wildlife from the alley. The squirrels were more active, and she saw several kinds of birds. Some of the yards had flowers, like hers. Others were weedy and overgrown.

A young boy about three or four squatted in the backyard of the fourth house on the right. He looked to be poking something in the mud. What? A bug maybe? She wanted to wave to him, but he kept his head down and never looked up. Maybe the next time she saw him she would try.

On the way home, she saw the boy again. This time he was playing with a small beachball, kicking it up into the air and trying to catch it. Just before she reached his house, he kicked the ball out of his fenced yard. Mariah ran to pick it up and took it to the boy's fence. "Is this yours?"

"Sorry."

"You don't need to be sorry. Here. What's your name?"

"Chick."

"As in chicken?"

"My mom says I looked like a grocery store chicken when I was little. She called me Chickpea until I got bigger."

"Well, it's nice to meet you, Chick. I hope to see you again sometime."

Chapter Eleven

Dick Hansen sat next to his wife as she lay in bed. Mostly he just watched Shianna breathe. It had been a long three years, trying to support the two of them while giving her the care she needed. Shianna had been a lively and energetic woman until she started having "the dropsies," as she called it. When they married, she was a dancer. She had been his love, his friend, and his partner until this disease had taken over. The two of them loved going on long walks and talking. Their conversations covered everything from the day's activities to situations at work to spiritual topics. Communication was the glue that held them together.

Shianna loved to twirl and leap in joy. Once, on a camping trip, Dick noticed how sure-footed she was walking across the slick rocks in the stream, how when she slipped, she was able to catch herself without missing a step.

Then, a year later, she began stumbling and shuffling her feet as if she were unsure of the next step. After innumerable visits to the doctors, they got the diagnosis—ALS. It took so long because doctors thought she was too young to have the disease. Gradually she lost more and more of her ability to move. Her speech was slow and awkward, making communication more difficult. For a while, she was in a wheelchair. Dick would still push her around on their walks until she finally couldn't sit up. He began feeding her, as she couldn't feed herself. Early on, when learning of her incurable disease, Shianna was adamant she did not want to be hooked up to a respirator. She put that in writing.

During that time, Dick did everything he could to maintain his real estate business while caring for his beloved wife. He tried to train as many agents as he could to keep the office afloat. A couple of "old timers" helped new agents learn the ropes, such as the subtle aspects of post-contract when the details had to be worked out for closing, but one retired and the other moved away. He started teaching real estate classes, both to supplement his income and to recruit talented prospects.

As Shianna became weaker and weaker, he couldn't spend much time away from her and the business suffered. Without supervision and encouragement, new agents either left for another office or just never showed up to work.

And now, Shianna couldn't even speak. Recently, she had difficulty swallowing and required a feeding tube. Dick's time was spent bathing her, talking to her, and just watching her breathe. To give one last set of classes, he had to bring in a caregiver while he was away. He didn't want to do this. He wanted to spend every bit of time he could with Shianna for fear that it would be the last moment of her existence.

That was the class Mariah took. She stood out to him, not because she was particularly attractive or charismatic, but mostly because she paid attention in class and asked appropriate questions. He knew she was going to pick up the material and actually use it. And he discovered how easy she was to talk to. Oh, how he craved good conversation! He decided to recruit Mariah, whatever it took.

And now here she was working in his office. He told Shianna about how he finally felt he had someone there he could count on. Shianna looked back into his eyes. Her face made little jerks and contractions like she wanted to talk but couldn't make it happen. He had a sense that she was appreciative or maybe he just interpreted it that way. He satisfied his need to communicate by looking into her eyes.

Dick's phone rang. It was Mariah. "Am I supposed to also be a psychological counselor? Gretchen is still publicly grieving, and Harry is fawning all over her in sympathy. It's sucking all the energy out of the office. What should I do? I've already suggested they go out and sell some real estate or check on their listings or something."

"You're right on track, Mariah. Tell her the office is for real estate business and to grieve at home."

"Sounds kind of harsh for someone grieving, but on the other hand ... for a leather couch?"

"Those two are newbies. They are a bit insecure about getting started and are probably attracted to anything that will distract them from doing the work. Try to reduce Harry's encouragement of Gretchen's howling by giving him a new lead."

The next walk-in came at two in the afternoon. The two men, obviously a couple, were perfect for Harry, and Mariah was confident they would all hit it off.

That left Gretchen's crying a little softer until Marla showed up. A large woman with a big personality, she swung her huge belly around as a weapon. After introducing herself to Mariah, she walked back to the agents' room. Gretchen's wail increased until Marla asked what was wrong. Gretchen told her all about the ruined sofa and started bawling again.

"Oh, stick a slipcover on it and go back to work!" Mariah heard Marla say. "If you sell enough real estate, you can buy yourself a new one."

"Marla's right," said Mariah. "Gretchen, it would do you good to get out and prospect. It could get your mind off the couch."

Gretchen tightened her fists and stared right at Mariah. "You don't understand how much this hurts! I feel like I've been raped!"

At that, Mariah's rage boiled over. "Obviously, you've *never* been raped—and to suggest a similarity is an insult to those who have!" Mariah's face was the color of Gretchen's red nails as she ran to the bathroom and slammed the door. Tears streamed down her face and onto her blouse. It took twenty minutes to calm down and clean herself up. When she finally came out of the bathroom, thankfully, Gretchen was gone.

It had been a long stressful day, and Mariah had not made it to the park in the morning like she had promised herself. She headed there now. It was not quite dusk, and the park looked foggy and mysterious. She made one loop around the flat part and then sat on a bench. It was a good time of day for introspection.

Mariah hated feeling like a victim, out of control over her life. It was hard to even see the good things that had come her way because so many bad things had happened. Even getting the rental house was hard to celebrate. She felt like a kept woman, even though Dick had never come on to her in that way. And now the office felt like an uncomfortable drama studio, and she didn't have the tools to manage it. She wanted to run away and leave it all behind, but that's what she did when she left Ohio. Was she the kind of person who runs away when the going gets tough? No! She just didn't understand why bad things happened to her when she thought she was doing the right things. *Obviously, there is no such thing as God, and the universe is not intelligent. Life is a crapshoot!* She wanted to talk to Alex.

"Well, hello again!"

Mariah startled. "Oh, I didn't expect to see you here at this hour."

"I didn't expect to see me here either," said Alex. "For some reason, I had this urgent feeling I needed to come."

"I'm glad to see you, actually. I've got a lot on my mind, and it doesn't feel too good."

"Having a lot on your mind never does feel good in my experience. Are you homeless now?"

"No," said Mariah, "and I'm not jobless, either. But it still worries me."

"Looking the gift horse in the mouth?"

"I guess. I took some real estate classes a while ago, and I went to see the teacher. He had asked me to come. I thought he was going to try to convince me to sell real estate out of his office, which I can't do. I can't afford to wait for a closing. But instead, he offered me a job in the office and free rent on a house he owns if I manage his other rentals. I don't know what the catch is and I'm afraid to find out."

"Anything else? So far it sounds like a lovely dream to me."

"He's never there, and I think he expects me to manage the place. I have no experience with this at all. Plus, all this drama stuff is going on with the agents. I don't have a title that would give me the authority to tell them what to do, but they need someone to kick their ass!"

"That sounds interesting. Why is he never there?"

"They say he has a sick wife he can't leave. She's dying."

"Well, I'd say that's a pretty good excuse for not coming in," Alex said with a smile. "Do you practice gratitude at all?"

"What do you mean by *practice* gratitude?"

Alex leaned back against the bench. "I spend some time every day in gratitude for each little thing I can think of. If I'm having a bad day, I'm just grateful for the way my shoes and socks warm my feet, that sort of thing. One grateful thing, however small, leads to another, and pretty soon gratitude swells and I can't help but be happy."

"I'm just so disappointed in the way life is turning out. I thought I was starting an exciting new job, with an apartment and new friends. Instead, I was attacked, raped, and out of a job. And now I don't even see my friends anymore. They're clear across town. I think I'm grieving."

"In my experience, grieving usually involves a feeling that something has been taken away. That something is actually what you need to give to yourself. Does that make any sense?"

"No, not really. I thought I was making progress toward a happy and secure life, and now that all seems to be gone. I think my situation is a lot worse than most."

"Like how?"

"Someone at the office has been crying for days over a rip in her leather couch and she had the gall to say she felt raped! I got so mad at her for saying that, I had to leave the room."

"Your thoughts are what give you the feeling of happiness and security, not your circumstances. Remember how I was suicidal over my situation? And here I am now, as happy as can be in the exact same situation. What I changed was my thinking. The magnitude of the problem doesn't determine how miserable our thinking can make us. For any circumstance, a change of thinking is the remedy."

Mariah slumped. "I don't know how to change my thinking. I guess I'm stuck with an unhappy brain."

"If you say so. I'll just leave you with this: What is one tiny thing you can be grateful for?"

"The last thought I had before you showed up was that I wanted to talk to you. You materialized immediately. I'm grateful for that. Are you a real person?"

"I'm more real than you can imagine."

Chapter Twelve

The gardens around Mariah's house were picture-perfect. Arthur was vigilant with the weeding, so the house looked like a showplace. Mariah found such pleasure just sitting in the backyard soaking it all in. She made sure to compliment Arthur on the nice job he was doing with the landscaping. Arthur only nodded and looked away.

Mariah asked him if he would like to take over the landscape maintenance of some other properties. He shrugged and said if they were close by, he might, but he had no car. So Mariah started him on some of the nearby rentals. The payment was small but helped him with his rent.

Two weeks after Mariah had moved, a bundle of forwarded mail arrived—the final electric bill and some twice-forwarded mail from Ohio made up most of it. When she got to the last two envelopes she gasped. One was from a hospital and the other from an ambulance service. She opened them with trembling fingers and spread them out on the table. She was unaware that ambulance services even charged people when the police were the ones who called them, and the hospital bill took her breath away. It was greater than her annual income by far!

She called the ambulance company and asked why they sent her the bill if she didn't call the ambulance. They replied that as she was unconscious, they had to take her to the hospital. Mariah felt faint and lay down on her bed. Sombra sat right on top of her, purring and kneading her chest. She rolled over and spent most of the day there in fetal position. It felt impossible to cope with yet another setback.

The next morning Mariah headed to the park. Walking on the hills helped dissipate her frustration, but her mind was still spinning with existential fear. At the end of the walk, just as she was getting into her car, she spotted Alex and walked over.

"Hi, Mariah, how are things going?"

"Not so good right now. I just got my hospital bill. I might have to declare bankruptcy or go to jail or something. The bill is way more than I will make in a year—or two, even."

"Ouch," said Alex. "Didn't you have any insurance?"

"No, I was on a temporary assignment when I was attacked. And then after the hospital stay, there wasn't enough work for me to come back."

"I think I can help you with that. You were at Vanderbilt, right?"

"Right."

"Good! I do a lot of volunteer work at that hospital, and I know some people who might be able to work out financial assistance or a payment plan."

"Wow, thanks, Alex. Can we do that right away?"

"I have some volunteer work coming up this afternoon. Would you like to meet me at the hospital around one?"

"That would be great!"

Alex walked Mariah over to the Vanderbilt financial office and introduced her to Justice, who helped Mariah with the application forms for both assistance and a payment plan. Alex took off for her volunteer work, leaving Mariah with Justice, who patiently helped Mariah fill in the paperwork.

"It takes weeks to work through the red tape," said Justice, "so I advise you to ignore the statements that will come in the mail and wait for the final decisions."

"Thank you, Justice, I am so grateful to you for helping me."

The business was accelerating at Dick Hanson Realty. Marla had several closings coming up, and even Mark was working on a couple of sales. Mariah referred some people to Clara, who also cleverly found her own prospects through cold-calling and walking the neighborhoods. That left Harry and Gretchen. Their inexperience caused them to lose a few potential sales, but they were game to keep trying. Mariah reminded them to prequalify buyers before viewing houses. She was glad to be able to help them.

Each day, when Mariah walked to work, she noticed Chick in his backyard. He seemed so thin and lifeless. He rarely looked up at her, and when he did, his big plaintive eyes and his gaunt face pulled at her heartstrings. When she called out to say hello, he often looked back at his house as if he was worried someone would notice him talking to her. He almost always wore the same filthy clothing. Mariah was sure he was being neglected and wondered if he ever got enough to eat. She started packing extra sandwiches in her lunch in case she could share them with Chick. On one occasion, when Chick was playing close to the back fence, Mariah was able to stand right next to him.

"Hi, Chick, how are you this morning?"

Chick shrugged and continued to play with a praying mantis he had found.

"Are you hungry? I have an extra sandwich today. Would you like it?"

He looked back at the house, fear showing in his face.

"I'll tell you what, Chick. I'll just put this sandwich through the fence, and you can eat it if you're hungry, or if you're not hungry you can just leave it there." Then she walked on to work.

One afternoon Mariah was alone in the office, and someone called wanting to look at houses with his wife. She told him she would meet with them around two-thirty. She called Dick immediately. "What should I do if no agent is here this afternoon?"

Dick reminded her that she had a real estate license and that she could lock up the office and take them out. Then he remembered Mariah's car with the faded paint and stuffed animals in the back. "Come over to my house and take my car to the office with you. You can show them around in that."

Mariah was flustered but realized Dick was right about not putting clients in her clunker. When Nancy and Robert arrived, Mariah talked with them for some time about what they wanted, as well as their target price range. They were in their early thirties. She noted that since Robert was in a fast-paced management position, where he was likely to be transferred frequently, an adjustable-rate mortgage would be a good fit for them. And with lower introductory interest payments, he could afford a higher house price. They looked at some listings, and Mariah quickly got the showings set up and the three set off in Dick's car. They saw the perfect house on the second showing. Nancy and Robert both complimented Mariah on how she had listened so well to what they wanted that she had been able to target the best houses right away. After some back and forth with the seller's agent, both parties agreed on a contract. Mariah was excited but also aware of the work ahead.

She returned Dick's car and told him the good news. Dick thought she could probably handle one sale at a time while still working in the office. He suggested placing more advertisements to bring in enough leads to generate clients for everyone.

Mariah called Dar to see if they could celebrate together. Dar wasn't available for dinner but suggested a Sunday brunch. It was a Seventh-Day Adventist buffet near the Vanderbilt University campus. The vegetarian restaurant served all sorts of delicious dishes Mariah had never tried before, such as fruit lasagna. They filled their plates and settled on a small table in a quiet corner to catch up on their lives.

Dar had passed her exams, of course. She was now looking for a good internship.

"Are you going to intern at Jackson & Veronne?" asked Mariah.

"No, I'm looking for an internship with someone in the state senate."

"Why? Didn't you want to keep working at J&V?"

"Not hardly. When I am finished here, I'd like to move to Washington D.C."

"To be a politician?"

"To work with government at some level. I'd like to be in a position to have a positive impact on the world.

Maybe working in an environmental agency. I'll be leaving an opening at Jackson & Verrone. Are you interested in coming back?"

"I'm just getting settled into my new job. The pay is small, but it comes with free rent on a house and the opportunity to sell some real estate on the side. I'm not sure I would be ready to go back again. Besides, to be honest, I didn't love working there either—or the pace."

"Oh, hey! We were meeting to celebrate your house sale. Congratulations!" Dar jumped up and grabbed both their cups to refill them with tea. "Cheers!"

"Thanks," said Mariah. "I hope everything goes well until closing. I think I'm finally back on the manifestation train with this sale. And I'll need it. Now I owe the hospital more than a year's salary. And that's if they give me a reduction or a payment plan."

"That's terrible," said Dar. "What are you going to do?

"I have to wait until I get the payment plan from the hospital. And then I hope I can get some real estate closings, like this sale we're celebrating, to augment my tiny salary."

The two women marveled at how all three friends were leaving Jackson & Verrone. Mariah had thought her two friends were permanent fixtures there and had patterned her plans to what they were doing. Funny how things change so quickly.

Three times, Mariah had left food for Chick through the fence. Each time, the sandwiches had been eaten and the plastic wrap had appeared on the alley side of the fence for Mariah to pick up. She felt they'd established good non-verbal communication. After the fourth day of doing this, she passed by Chick's yard and saw him crying on the back porch. It was not a loud cry, but she could tell he was sobbing. His chest heaved and he cradled his left hand. Was that blood she saw? "Chick, what's wrong?" she shouted. When he didn't respond, she said, "Come here! I can help you." He slowly meandered toward the back fence, moaning.

"Let's have a look at this. Can you show me where you are hurt?" He turned his left hand, and Mariah could see a cut between his thumb and forefinger. It looked fairly deep. He must have been bleeding for some time, as there was a lot of dried blood around his hand. "Chick, you need to get this cleaned up and bandaged. Is your mother home?"

"No. She went out."

"You mean she left you here all alone?"

"I know how to feed myself. Mostly I open these cans of pork and beans. But this time my hand slipped."

"I have first aid supplies at my house. Can you come over to my house?"

"No, I'm not supposed to leave."

"Okay, I'll bring them to you."

Mariah fetched the supplies from her bathroom. She carried them to Chick's house and knocked on the front door. No one answered, so she attempted to open the door, but it was locked. She tried walking around to the fenced yard. The front and side of the landscape were overgrown and weedy. Some of the large shrubbery caught her clothing, and it was an effort to unsnag her way around the house. She finally found the gate, which was not locked, so she let herself through. Chick was still hunched on the back porch.

"We need to wash this first," said Mariah. Once it's cleaned up, I'll bandage your cut." Chick balked when Mariah tried to enter the house with him. "We need water to wash your hand, Chick." He just stood outside silently crying. Tears streamed down his cheeks. Mariah looked around for a water spigot and finally found one behind some old dead potted plants. "Come here, Chick, and we'll wash your hand." Fortunately, she had remembered to bring liquid soap and some peroxide. Chick was amazingly stoic as she washed both his hands and then poured some peroxide over the cut to sterilize it. She covered the cut with antibiotic ointment and wrapped his whole hand with gauze. Since the cut was in the web between his thumb and finger, there wasn't much real estate on his hand for a smaller bandage. When she was done, Chick murmured, "Thank you," and Mariah took her tools home and headed to work two hours late.

She couldn't stop thinking about Chick. His situation—being left alone, having to open cans of beans by himself for food, and his fear of even talking to outsiders—confirmed her conclusion that Chick was a criminally neglected child. What should she do about it? She wished she could take him home with her, even though she knew it would be inappropriate. But children all deserved a loving family; not a mom who was never around and no dad, apparently. Mariah's heart ached for him. The brave little boy was trying to take care of himself without complaint. She wondered if she should call Family and Children's Services to report it, but she had read too many stories of foster homes being harsh environments.

The rest of the day was busy at Dick Hansen Realty. The phone rang constantly, and many people dropped in. Mariah had her hands full passing prospects to various agents. She didn't feel that she could take any prospects herself. Her contract with Nancy and Robert was moving along. Robert's adjustable-rate mortgage application was quickly approved.

Two weeks had gone by without any problem, and then Mariah's phone rang. It was Robert.

"Bad news, Mariah," said Robert.

"What?"

"My company just informed me I'm being relocated to Texas."

"Oh, no! What about the contract, then?"

"I know we'll have to forfeit the earnest money, but we need to get out of the contract."

Mariah felt her face get cold. She called Dick.

Dick suggested she call the seller's agent and see what they could work out. Luckily the seller's agent had two back-up contracts and would even be willing to refund half the earnest money if another contract was finalized quickly.

That was a relief for Nancy and Robert's sake but was still bad news for Mariah. She had planned to use some of the commission to pay for the ambulance service and buy a new couch. She left work late, feeling like a failure.

It was almost dark, so she walked on the lit street, rather than the alley. As she approached her block, she saw several police cars with flashing lights. It seemed to be in front of Chick's house. When she got closer several people were standing around just outside of the police action.

"What's happening?" Mariah asked.

"The next-door neighbor called the police on a couple who were arguing loudly. The man was beating the woman, and they could hear the screams. When the police arrived, they took the man into custody. He's in that second car up there."

At that moment an ambulance pulled up and the emergency medical technicians went directly into the house with a stretcher. Minutes later they exited with a woman strapped in the gurney. After loading her in, the ambulance took off with its lights on and siren wailing.

Mariah approached one of the officers. "What about Chick?" she asked.

"Ma'am, we don't handle pets."

"No, Chick is a little four-year-old boy who lives here. You can't just leave him alone."

The policeman got on his radio and asked the men still looking through the house to check for a small child, probably in the backyard.

"What will they do with him?" she asked.

"We'll take him into the precinct office with us and ask him some questions and then transfer him to Children's Services."

Going home, Mariah couldn't stop thinking about Chick. She decided to call the police station to see how he was doing. Three phone calls later she finally connected with the right precinct office. The desk person told her they had Chick and were trying to question him, but he wasn't talking. They had already called Children's Services to pick him up.

"What about his mother? Are they going to give him back to his mother?"

"The mother was pronounced dead at the hospital."

Stunned, Mariah put down the phone. Poor Chick. She wanted to wrap her arms around him and promise him that life would treat him better in the future. She prayed he would be given a stable family with a mother and father who loved him. He deserved it.

The next morning Mariah dragged herself into the bathroom. The mirror was not her friend. She usually avoided looking at herself. But that Saturday morning as she was leaving the bathroom, something caught her eye that made her stop and take a closer look. Her hair was growing back on the left side. She had been parting it on the right to cover up the scars. That worked for a while but now her hair seemed shaggy and just plain wrong. She decided to cut it all the same length and just wear a short bob. She also noticed that her face looked fuller than before. It was time to admit she had gained at least twenty pounds!

Mariah headed to the nearest walk-in hair stylist. After discussing the problem and possible solutions, Samantha began cutting. As she worked, they chatted, and the subject of weight gain came up.

"I don't know why I gained so much weight! I don't eat any more than I always have," said Mariah. "I often don't even feel like eating."

"Are you sure you're not pregnant?"

Mariah looked stunned. She hadn't thought about that possibility since being tested at the Public Health Department. "Do I look pregnant?"

"There's a certain look that women get when they're pregnant. It shows up sometimes even before they find out. It's a kind of softening all over. Maybe it's even their aura. Anyway, I usually know when someone is pregnant, and I thought you were."

Mariah quietly paid for her haircut and left the shop. She wasn't angry at the hairdresser, but shocked, as if she had been hit with a brick.

She didn't want to think about it. The hairdresser could be wrong. Whoever heard of the hairdresser pregnancy test, anyway?

Early Sunday morning, with her eyes still closed, she thought about her day and whether she would go to the park. It felt so good just to lie there in a half-awake state; maybe she would remain for another hour. Then she noticed a strange feeling like butterflies in her pelvic region. Three or four times the butterflies tickled her insides. As she lay there, the reality of a living being inside her sunk in. It was real. And it was alive. Would she get rid of it?

On one hand, it was a living being in its own right—and a part of her. On the other, it was a thing caused by a man she didn't know. Someone who had brutally imposed this upon her. She wanted to get rid of him, get rid of *it* because of what it represented. Last January, when she had gone to the Health Authority for the test and revealed she'd been raped, the nurse had mentioned abortion. Is it still an option? Abortion didn't feel right. It might be painful. And expensive. It was much more difficult to imagine her life after an abortion than it was to imagine letting this thing live. But, if she went ahead and had the child, she'd be a slave to it. Her life would be turned upside down with the new responsibilities, even more than it had already been. And without a partner, would she resent it? Might seeing the child every day remind her of the man who did this? She could give the baby up for adoption, but then why go through the whole pregnancy?

Mariah got up. She pulled on her jeans, exhaled a long breath and, while holding it, quickly tried to fasten the top button before taking the next breath. *How long will I be wearing these clothes?*

Her mind moved back to abortion. The idea of a doctor invading her body almost felt like a second rape. And she already had more hospital bills than she could ever pay off. How could she afford an abortion?

Mariah walked around her house trying to decide what to do. No decision was good. A part of her felt the excitement of a spark of life inside her. Another part was filled with fear. Who was this man who impregnated her? Would she be carrying his bad energy around? Was the embryo a "bad seed?" Or was it an innocent being?

Unable to deal with the situation, she shoved those thoughts to the back of her mind and began to focus on living one day at a time.

Chapter Thirteen

The days were long for Dick Hansen. Shianna was losing her ability to breathe. The struggle was excruciating to watch. Dick continued to bathe her and feed her through the tube. He talked to her a lot, hoping it would take her attention away from the constant battle. To keep the house bright and cheerful, he kept the curtains open in the daytime. He would stand at the window and describe to Shianna everything he saw happening outside. She knew every squirrel family and bird in the area. She knew in detail the stories of the children who played outside the house.

Dick's daily routine was to wash Shianna in the bed and roll her over from one side to the other, eventually replacing the old, soiled bedding with new. Then he would massage her muscles and smooth lotion over her skin to keep it in good health. He moved her arms and legs for her to relieve the discomfort of being in the same position for hours. He could tell when a spasm caused her pain, and he would massage the offending muscle.

On this particular day, Shianna was not as cooperative as usual. When he moved her, she fought and whimpered. Dick did the minimum exercise with her and only massaged her a little. He thought her breathing was shallower. He spent the afternoon talking to her before preparing her tube feeding.

Shianna moaned and shook her head as much as she could to indicate she did not want the food. Dick left her alone for a while to make his daily call to Mariah.

Dick and Mariah usually talked about what was going on in the office and he always wanted every detail. After covering work, as their association grew, they moved to more personal aspects of life. Eventually, Mariah asked what it was like for Dick to be there with Shianna as she was dying.

"There are plenty of things for me to do here," said Dick. "I have to be the one to care for both our bodies. I bathe and feed both of us—just about everything a body does, I do for both myself and Shianna. But I want to be here with her and I'm grateful for every last second I can have with the woman I love."

"There's that gratitude thing again," she whispered.

"Gratitude thing?"

"You just said you were grateful for your time with Shianna. Funny thing, that was exactly what my friend Alexandria said I should do. Practice gratitude. I thought she just didn't understand how bad my life was to suggest practicing gratitude as an antidote."

"It's always a choice," said Dick. "I could be sad that this is happening to Shianna and angry that my wife can no longer enjoy the things we used to, or I can choose to think about how grateful I am that I had a chance to know her when she was active. I think the gratitude drowns out the depressing thoughts."

"I can't think of a way to have gratitude that I'm pregnant or that I have a hospital bill that's more than I will make in a year or two."

"You're pregnant?"

"From the rape. You know, when I was attacked and ended up in the hospital."

After a long pause, Dick said wistfully, "I had always wanted to have children before this happened with Shianna."

"I want to have a family, too—with a loving husband. I wasted four years with a guy before he dumped me. And now I'm pregnant from a rapist. This is not the way I wanted my life to go. That's why it's so difficult for me to be grateful."

"All the more reason to practice gratitude. Instead of trying to tell life how you want it to work for you, collect all the things you can think of to be grateful for."

"I'll try."

"Talk to you tomorrow," said Dick.

"Bye."

Dick returned to Shianna's room and sat in the green easy chair next to her bed. He reached out and slipped his hand into hers and closed his eyes. He prayed an inner prayer of gratitude and fell asleep.

Mariah sat on the ledge of the retaining wall in her backyard. Okay, here goes, she thought. I'm grateful for this nice backyard. And for Arthur, who keeps it looking so nice. That felt good. Of course, I'm grateful for this house to live in rent-free. Then she smiled and shouted, "I'm grateful not to have to wear those high heels anymore!"

At about two-thirty in the morning, Dick awoke. He was still in the chair next to Shianna. Looking around in the dimness of the night light, he reached out to take Shianna's hand once more, which was still where it was when he fell asleep. It was cold. A shiver ran through his body as he realized what it meant. Although he knew this was coming, he still felt stunned. He walked back and forth at the foot of her bed and then paced around the whole house. He tried to review what he needed to do next, but his brain wasn't cooperating; and every time he came up with one detail, his brain went on strike and wouldn't let him flesh it out. He couldn't go to bed, even though it was the middle of the night. He sat back down in the chair and spent the rest of the night staring, thoughtless.

Thankfully, they had planned months prior as to Shianna's wishes upon her death. Dick had a list of the people to notify and invite to her funeral. Shianna had always called it a wake and wanted people to be in a celebratory mood. She had even written her own obituary as a fun exercise when she had first gotten her diagnosis.

After the light had returned to the sky, Dick called the funeral home to pick up Shianna's body. Then he called Arlett, Shianna's mother. Shianna and her mother had argued at the time she was diagnosed with ALS. They had heated disagreements over the choices her daughter was making regarding the progression of her illness and end of life. The arguments had become so heated that the two cut off all communication. So now Dick had to make the call.

"Hello, Arlett? This is Dick."

After a long pause, she said, "So it's over now."

"Yes."

"Are you having a funeral?"

"Yes, and I ... and I'd like you to come if you choose to."

"Coffin?"

"No, you know Shianna wanted to be cremated."

Dick heard a click and then a dial tone.

He sighed.

His next move was to make the arrangements for the wake, though he felt overwhelmed by his situation and the number of tasks he faced. Dick had few ideas for places he could use to accommodate the many people who would want to honor Shianna. The country club was a good possibility, but it was expensive. Next, he called the Tennessee State Performing Arts Program, where Shianna had danced before she got sick. Several of her contacts were still there and were on the invitation list. Sure enough, one of Shianna's old professors was glad to hear from Dick, although sad to hear the reason. He offered to book a space in one of the larger studios. Dick gratefully accepted.

Needing a break from talking to people, he stripped Shianna's bedding, vacuumed the floor, and boxed up all the paraphernalia for the body that was no longer there. Then he sat back in the chair beside the bed and closed his eyes. He was hoping to sense Shianna in spirit. Perhaps he would have a vision of the woman he loves, but he quickly fell asleep. He dreamed of a beautiful tapestry he seemed to have created. One strand of yarn was pulling out. He began trying to remove the bad string, causing it to ravel out even more. He tried desperately to save the tapestry but couldn't find a strong enough yarn to fix it. Then he felt himself disappearing until he had no sense of his being. But it was not he who had died.

Dick was awake now but still pondering the dream. *Is that what death is like?* The lack of being he experienced in the dream was itself freeing and at the same time frightening. Who was he without an identity? Clearly, the dream was telling him he could not move forward without letting go of his joint identity with Shianna. He didn't want to. He had let go of his own identity to put his entire focus on Shianna—her health, her needs, and remembering who she had been. The hole in his chest would not close. He would walk through the rest of his life as a human doughnut.

Amused at that thought, with a lighter spirit, he went back to work on planning and making all the phone calls. He contacted Shianna's favorite musicians and asked them to play at the wake. He worked back and forth between the musicians and the room scheduler until he found a mutually agreeable date. He called a caterer and arranged for the food and drink.

Dick called Mariah for the evening check-in. "Shianna passed away last night," he said.

"I'm sorry, Dick. Is there anything I can do to help?"

"Not right at the moment. I think I've found a friend to address the invitations to the wake. I'm having them printed today. It's coming together pretty quickly because of all the planning we did when Shianna was alive. I want you to come to the wake. There will be lots of people you should meet."

"Okay. Will you be coming into the office more now?"

"Not right away. I still have to work out a lot of details, and I need some time to myself to process."

"Understood. I look forward to when you do come in. The office feels a little stale right now. We're waiting for closings and nothing new has happened."

Stale. That word reminded Dick how much energy the office had lost while he was away. His enthusiasm was missing. Dick loved real estate. That's why he became a broker and why he taught classes and why he enjoyed encouraging new people in the business. Real estate was in his DNA. Dick's father was a builder. He got Dick into real estate sales at an early age to sell the houses his father built. Now he would put more of himself back into the business. He would find his wholeness again. At the end of the day, he settled into the green chair he had spent so much time in with Shianna and wept.

Three weeks passed quickly as Dick prepared for the wake. Shianna's friends were mostly involved in the arts of some type. Musicians, dancers, visual artists, and patrons of the arts were all eager to help Dick.

At the designated hour, people began to arrive. The band was already playing. There was an open mic on the stage where people could come up and say a few words about Shianna whenever the spirit moved them. Tables were loaded with food and drink, with only a few chairs sprinkled around randomly, as people were mostly expected to stand or dance.

The room was already full when Mariah entered. She was wearing a flowing long dress that beautifully accommodated her growing belly. It was a green print with tiny pink flowers and a shirred bodice that was starting to fill out with her enlarging bust. At first, she felt strange because she didn't know anyone, but eventually, she noticed a few people from the office and even some from Jackson & Verrone. Mariah said hello to them as she passed. Weaving between bodies, she noticed the unique odors of each individual—their shampoo, perfume, sweat—which blended into a fruity pungent cloud. Then halfway across the room, she spotted Alexandria's beautiful golden locks. Mariah wound her way around clusters of people and food tables to approach her.

"Alex, hi, I didn't expect to see you here."

"Oh, yes, Shianna and I were good friends—and Dick was the listing agent on our new house, as well as handling the sale of our old one."

"So did you know it was Dick Hansen that I was working for all along?"

"I don't think you named him, but I knew all the same. How is it going for you?"

"I like it so far. I enjoy listening to the customers and then solving the puzzle of what houses on the market and financing options would fit their needs. It feels creative to do that. I'm hoping to find more people to work with. And I wanted to tell you—I'm focused on practicing gratitude now. Thank you for that advice. Dick encouraged me in that direction, too. It's an amazing tool."

"I'm glad it helped. Not only does gratitude raise spirits, but it also clears the path to recognizing and receiving what we desire. By the way, I might have a couple I could refer to you. Let's talk sometime later." Then Alex waved to some people in the crowd and walked toward them.

Dick joined Mariah, but at the same moment, someone went up to the microphone to tell a story about how he met Shianna and how much she meant to him. When he was finished, Dick said, "I see you found Alex. She's a kick, isn't she? Lots of people here are in the music business and supporters of the arts. Introduce yourself to folks you don't know, and I think you'll be surprised at how friendly they are. You might even get some leads for real estate deals. Just tell them you are an agent in my office."

Mariah followed Dick's suggestion and by the end of the evening, in addition to meeting many interesting people, she had the names and phone numbers of three prospects who wanted to talk to her more about real estate. And that was in addition to the referral promised by Alex.

One thing she had failed to do was learn Alexandria's last name or a way to contact her.

Chapter Fourteen

Dick's house looked like a tornado had hit. Clothes piled on every possible surface. He was in the process of selecting and setting aside some of Shianna's things that brought special memories. He would put them in storage. The rest could go to Goodwill. Once he had separated and packed, he started looking at his closet. Shianna had picked out a lot of his clothing with colors that appealed to her. Dick loved how bright and cheerful her color choices were, but in truth, they didn't feel like him. He moved them around so that some of his old favorite plaid shirts and khaki pants were closer to the front.

Then he pulled down some of the organza room dividers and poofy curtains. He'd buy new ones and also paint the rooms. Blue, green, and beige seemed much more his colors than the pink, purple, and silver that Shianna had chosen. Strangely, he did not feel disloyal. He felt guided.

After driving the boxes to Goodwill, it was time to check in with Mariah. With some things taken care of, he felt ready.

"How are things going in the office?"

"I don't know, they seem okay."

"Any closings coming up?"

"One. Clara has a small house closing this week. And Mark keeps claiming that he's going to get an instant listing and closing for cash. We'll see."

"I'd give Mark the benefit of the doubt. He's a wheeler dealer. What about you? Have you called some of the contacts you got at the wake?"

"I called one. She said she was not ready to talk about selling, but she just wanted to know someone she could call on later."

"That's the kind of person you can cultivate. Get to know her. Maybe she knows others in the neighborhood who want to sell. You could also run the comps for her if she wants to know what her house might be worth."

"All right, I could do that, but I didn't feel like it was going to go anywhere right away."

"Here's another tip, Mariah. Whenever you call on someone and it feels flat, call another lead immediately. And keep doing that until you can leave the telephone on a high note emotionally. Otherwise, you end up stuck in the doldrums."

"I know what you mean. I think I'm in the doldrums now. Do you have Alex's phone number? And her last name? I have been meeting her in the park and I never got that information."

"Sure, no problem. And call her right away. She is usually full of great information and knows a lot of people."

Mariah didn't call Alex right away. She was afraid to bother her in the evening and felt uncomfortable using this new method of reaching her.

The next morning, she went to the park for her walk hoping she would see Alex there. The one-mile loop was getting easier, even as she was gaining weight in her belly. By the top of the hill, she had a relaxed rhythm that made her feel good all over. Coming down to the park entrance, she decided to do some stretches the way Alex does. As she finished, she looked up to see her friend standing over her with a big smile.

"Alex! I was hoping I would see you today. In fact, I wanted to call you last night, but I was afraid to bother you."

Still smiling, Alex said, "I would strongly suggest never to assume you know the state of mind of another person. What if I was thinking of you and wishing you would call?"

"Oh, I hadn't thought of that. How would I know if you wanted to talk to me?"

"That's the point! You call and ask."

"That sounds simple enough. I was hoping you'd be willing to say more about those contacts you mentioned at the wake."

"Exactly. I have some friends who are in the same situation I was when Dick worked with us. They need to sell their little house and buy a nice house in my neighborhood. They should get started right away, because I know someone in my neighborhood who is thinking about selling."

"Can you give me their contact information? I'll get in touch with them."

"Call me when I get home. I didn't bring it to the park."

Deep in thought, Mariah walked back to her car. The instructions she was getting from both Dick and Alex were alien to her old way of thinking. She wasn't used to being so forward, so proactive. What she did have, though, was the ability to follow directions, so as soon as she got home, she put in a call to Alex to get the phone number. Once armed with the contact information, Mariah called the person immediately.

"Hello, Joanne? This is Mariah McKenzie from Dick Hansen Real Estate. "Alexandria Goodchild gave me your number. Is this a good time for us to talk?"

"I guess so, as good as any."

"I understand you need to sell your house?"

"Well, yes. We're getting a big chunk of royalty money and want to put it and our equity in this house into a larger, nicer house. It will help with our taxes if we take the profits from selling our house and roll it into the new property."

"When do you hope this will take place?"

"By next month, actually."

"Okay, then we need to get started right away. I could come over this evening to take measurements and then get a proposal to you by tomorrow. Would that work?"

"What time this evening? I have to go out. I'll be leaving at six."

"No problem. I can stop by at four-fifteen and be finished in plenty of time."

Mariah sat on the back retaining wall with a smile on her face reveling in the happy feeling that it went so well with Joanne. *Gratitude is easy when things are going well*, she thought. She bounced up with a skip and felt some strong kicks from the little being inside her belly. Attempting to hold onto her happy state, she doubled down on gratitude, crowding out a flash of anxiety.

It was almost ten o'clock as Mariah started her short morning walk to the office.

When she got there, things seemed different. For one thing, all the agents were there. And for another, Dick's office door was closed. Mariah took her usual place at the front desk and started looking at house listings and closings in Joanne's neighborhood. It seemed like a comfortable, solid community of small brick homes with well-kept yards.

Finally, Dick's office door opened and someone she had never seen before came out with a smile. Dick followed her out and introduced her to Mariah as a new agent, Roxanne, who would be starting to work in the office. Mariah's first impression was that she looked like a Barbie doll blown up to human size. She was rather tall, probably about five feet, ten inches but looked even taller with the four-inch heels. She was slender with a large bust and a tiny waist emphasized by a wide gold belt. Her full head of red hair was carefully coiffed. Mariah smiled with amusement but liked her immediately, responding to her personality. Dick explained that Roxanne had been a very successful realtor in Nebraska, where she had lived until recently moving to Nashville.

Dick stepped to the doorway of the realtors' room and asked Gretchen to come into his office. Not ten minutes after the door closed, the two emerged. Gretchen walked quickly to her desk, grabbed her belongings, and left. Puzzled, Mariah looked up at Dick. He returned her gaze and suggested she come into his office next.

"Now that I'm back in the office, the energy is going to have to improve. I'm asking each realtor how they feel about their work, the office, and what kind of energy they're willing to bring to it."

"So did you fire Gretchen?" asked Mariah.

"No, I didn't have to. I just asked her what her goals were and how she felt about creating a more productive atmosphere here. She told me she only came into the office to get away from her kids and decided to leave. Anyway, I don't hire and fire anyone because they're not actually employees."

"Except for me."

"Yes, you are the only employee here. And you are also an independent contractor. What are your thoughts about the office atmosphere and how we can improve it? I know you mentioned that things seemed a little stale at the moment."

Mariah took a minute to reply. "I think things have seemed a little slow and definitely stale, but personally, I'm getting pretty excited about doing more real estate work—not that I mind doing the office work, as well. I have a potential listing coming up. I have an appointment at four-fifteen with a client to measure the house, and I will give a proposal tomorrow."

"Nice!" said Dick. "I knew I could count on you."

Dick continued to invite each realtor into his office one by one. When he was done, Gretchen and Harry had both decided to leave, and everyone else had big smiles.

Dick came out and asked the crew what colors to paint the office interior. They came up with a nice light blue and apricot color scheme with dark green accents.

At four o'clock, Mariah headed out to measure Joanne's house. She had removed the stuffed animals from her clunker car and polished it the best she could, given the poor paint condition. Outfitted with a notepad and measuring tape, she calculated the square footage and promised Joanne she would stop by the next day to make her proposal. Then she headed back to the office to write up the listing particulars and run comparables to calculate a price.

Dick was still at his desk and gave her some more pointers on what to do next.

"As soon as you get the listing signed, go out to all the neighbors and tell them about it. Ask if they know anyone looking for a house in their neighborhood. Also, ask if they are interested in selling their house."

Tentatively, Mariah said, "Okay."

"You're not reluctant to do this, are you, Mariah?"

"I'm afraid people are going to ask me personal questions about being pregnant. What if they ask about the father?"

"Mariah, being pregnant makes you the most popular person in the real estate business. Everyone wants to talk to you. And they are always polite to a pregnant woman—you'll see."

"I guess I just don't feel so good about myself in this state," Mariah said.

After securing the listing the next day, she knocked on a few doors on either side of the house. One occupant wasn't there, and the other just said she didn't know any-one wanting to buy or sell a house. Mariah was tired and still reluctant. She wanted to go home.

Later, on her walk in the park, Mariah was obsessed with worry about her pregnancy showing and the shame she felt about it. She wanted to talk to Alex but didn't see her.

Chapter Fifteen

It was a warm morning. The temperature was expected to be in the eighties. Mariah sat outside in the backyard wearing her flimsiest blouse and a new pair of stretchy-front pants as she watched Arthur weeding and deadheading the flowers. Arthur was aware she was there but never looked back at her. In fact, since she had moved into the house, although they'd spoken, the two had never even made eye contact. A few minutes later, Mariah decided to try lying down on the ledge, hoping to find it comfortable.

Arthur finally looked back at Mariah and noticed her protruding belly. He let that sink in for a moment. Mariah stood up suddenly. "That sure was a mistake, trying to lie down on the ledge. I'll have to bring out some cushions."

Now Arthur was standing too and looking directly at Mariah's belly.

"I know what you're thinking," said Mariah, "and you are right. I'm pregnant."

"No, I just . . . never . . . saw. . . ."

"A man? There isn't one. I was raped."

"When?"

"Before I moved here."

Arthur looked horrified. "Did the police catch him?"

"No, I don't even know if they tried. I was unconscious and ended up in the hospital for days." Mariah then turned away and went back into her house.

Arthur was stunned. He wanted to know more—much more. When exactly did it happen, and where? This was their first personal conversation, and he wasn't sure how many more questions he could ask.

Mariah sat down at her kitchen table and grabbed a piece of stiff junk mail to fan herself. Why did she say that? She hadn't wanted to tell anybody, and there she was blabbing to Arthur, whom she hardly even knew!

By the time Mariah went back outside, Arthur had gone into his little apartment. Mariah paced around the yard, wondering if she could undo what she had already said. Finally, she knocked on Arthur's door. "Do you mind if I pick some of those roses to bring inside my house?"

"Sure. There's no need to ask, but I'll cut them for you."

Pruners and gloves in hand, Arthur walked with Mariah over to the bush and began carefully choosing the freshest blooms. "When is the baby due?" he asked as he handed her the roses.

"August 10th, I think." Mariah said, turning toward the house, "Thank you, I'm going to put these in water."

Arthur nodded. That fits the time frame, he thought. He had been having flashbacks from that day he was fired. He was never sure what parts were real and what parts were mixed in with memories from way back in his past. He knew he was drunk out of his mind. Now, despite his dread, he needed to know where Mariah was raped. He wasn't sure why, but he just couldn't leave it alone.

Later when the mail came, Mariah dumped it onto her little table, which was already piled up with letters that had been coming for weeks, much of them unopened. In fact, some of them were months old. After she had applied for financial help from the hospital, threatening bills kept coming and Justice had advised her to disregard them until she got a reply on her application for assistance and a payment plan.

The new mail contained a letter from the hospital. It looked different from the others, so Mariah decided to open it. Sure enough, it was the determination letter telling her the total bill was cut in half and there was now an almost affordable monthly payment. Relieved, she grabbed all the old bills and carried them out to the trash.

With a lighter step and a smile, she left for the office. She had work to do today for her new listing. The for-sale sign was up, and she had already planned an open house and placed the ads but needed to make flyers and distribute them before Sunday.

Arthur finished weeding the yard and carried the debris to the garbage. As he absent-mindedly lifted the lid, he spotted a pile of letters addressed to Mariah. Some of the letters from Vanderbilt Hospital were unopened. Arthur grabbed the stack and headed for his apartment. He began opening them. The earliest bill he found, already out of the envelope, showed the first charges. That would have been the date the rape happened. He nervously rummaged through the rest of the mail until he came to an ambulance service bill. Arthur trembled as he opened the envelope. It itemized the trip to the hospital from the corner of 5th and Deaderick, the very place where he had collapsed under the blinking streetlight. Now, his confusion and anxiety all began to make sense. Feeling faint, he quickly bundled up the papers and took them back to the can, hiding them under the weeds.

Back inside, he sat on his bed. His memories were all dark and patchy. There was no woman in those memories—just a symbol. A symbol of bossy women and blaming sisters. And an angry father. He had remembered flashes of his body going through the motions that could have been rape. He felt as if he were watching from outside himself like he was the little three-year-old crying under the table as he saw his father rape the housekeeper. Now he had a face to go with the symbol and it didn't match. Mariah had been nice to him, respectful, not like his old bosses or his sister or his mother. He swore not to look at her face again.

The hot afternoon made work at the real estate office difficult. The large whole-house fan didn't offer much relief. "The embryo" was moving a lot, kicking and jerking. Mariah still couldn't think of it as her baby. It was just a representation of her painful acceptance of victimhood.

She pushed through the afternoon, making flyers for the weekend. Finally, she finished her work, but it was still way too hot to go home. She had no appetite for dinner either, so she decided to drive to a place where she could enjoy some air conditioning. As she drove, she noticed a bookstore and wondered if that was where Alex browsed.

Entering, she looked for the section on self-help and spiritual books. She felt a figure standing behind her and whirled around to find herself face-to-face with Dick Hansen.

"Oh! I didn't expect to see you here!" she exclaimed.

"I spend a lot of time at this bookstore, especially on a hot day," he grinned.

"Isn't this where Alex browses too?"

"As a matter of fact, I introduced her to it."

"She told me she found the bookstore when she was depressed. She said it helped her get through some tough times."

Dick drew a long breath. "I sold Alex and her husband, Charlie, the house they live in now. I used to visit them periodically just to see how they were doing. A couple of years after they moved, I visited when Alex was really low, maybe suicidal. I had a long talk with her about depression and how it works and took her here to show her some books that I thought would help her."

"Amazing. This place must have some fantastic books to make that much difference to a person."

"Sure. Look for yourself," said Dick, "but it's not enough to just read them. You have to put the ideas into practice."

"Like gratitude?"

"Yeah, like gratitude. That's a good start. And then forgiveness when you're ready."

"Oh, that's a hard one. There are a few people I could never forgive. They don't deserve forgiveness!"

Dick tipped his head to the side. "Forgiveness is not for the other person. It's for *you*. Understand?"

"Not really. What do I need forgiveness for?"

"Mariah, how do you feel when you're condemning someone for doing something you think is bad?"

"Mad. My chest tightens. I feel like I want to strike them, but I can't."

"And what do you think they feel at that same moment?"

"Nothing, probably . . . I don't know."

"So? What would it take for you to feel better?"

"I see your point. But if I forgive them, then I'm letting what they did be okay."

"You know, as long as you hold on to these negative feelings, you are allowing the perpetrator to control how you feel inside your own body. Why would you want to give them that much control over you? Forgiveness helps you to disengage from an uncomfortable situation."

"Wow, Dick, I just don't feel ready for this."

"Why don't you sit with it for a while? Are you ready for your open house on Sunday?"

"I think so. I made some flyers and I'll walk the neighborhood with them tomorrow."

"Great. I know you'll have a good time."

Mariah wasn't expecting to have a good time on Saturday. Knocking on strangers' doors was alien to her. She thought they would be bothered by her intrusion. Nevertheless, she took the flyers to the neighborhood and began her rounds. Remarkably, people seemed pleasant. Some asked many questions about the house and the owners' plans. Occasionally a woman would ask her if she was expecting and seemed genuinely excited for her. No one was intrusive enough to ask about the circumstances of her pregnancy. By the time she'd distributed most of the flyers, she had met one other person in the neighborhood who might want to sell her house and several who wanted friends to come to the open house. Mariah was glad she had pushed herself to do this after all.

That evening she got an unexpected call from her friend Sara.

"Sara! I'm surprised to hear from you. What's up?"

"I just got back into town from a marvelous trip to Greece. We came home to Nashville for the weekend, but we'll be going on another trip on Monday. I have a friend I'd like you to meet. How about dinner?"

"I don't know. I have an open house coming up tomorrow and I need to get some rest."

"Aw, come on. Everybody has to eat. Are you dating someone now?"

"Oh, are you trying to set me up on a blind date?"

"Maybe. You once said you were afraid you'd never find love. You know how good I am at finding cute guys. I think you might hit it off. And if you don't like each other, then no big deal."

Mariah reluctantly decided to accept the dinner invitation, mostly so she could catch up on Sara's life.

Mariah met Sara and the two men at a quiet restaurant near downtown. Sara introduced her boyfriend, Pete, and their friend Sam. Sam looked at Mariah with direct eye contact. He was about six feet tall with a medium, muscular build and hair the same reddish-brown color as Mariah's. But what stood out the most were his penetrating hazel eyes locked on hers. After the four were seated, they began to have a lively conversation about Sara and Pete's travels and their plans to go to Peru. Sam lived in Nashville near Sara and Mariah's old apartments. He was into music and was trying to get established as a songwriter. He talked about all the music stars he had met and how cool they were. Mariah didn't have a strong interest in country music but listened to Sam's stories with amusement.

When Mariah got up to use the ladies' room, Sara went with her. In the restroom, Sara said, "Mariah, why didn't you tell me you were pregnant? What the heck?"

Mariah looked away, then finally, "You know what happened to me. This was the result."

"Didn't you think of getting an abortion or something?"

"I don't know. I was in the hospital for days, and then there was the snow. When I finally got a test, it was negative. By the time I realized I was actually pregnant, it was too late. Also, I had no job and a lot of hospital bills. I wouldn't have been able to pay for it."

"You poor thing. Life has been hard for you."

"You can say that again."

Once back at the table, Mariah said she needed to go home. "It's nice meeting you, Sam."

"Likewise," replied Sam. "I'll walk you to your car."

Mariah wasn't sure if she was more afraid of being accosted by some stranger on the way to her car or of Sam trying to force himself on her. She didn't answer one way or the other, so Sam followed along.

"I enjoyed our conversation tonight," said Sam as he put his arm over her shoulder. Again, his hazel eyes locked onto hers and Mariah felt uncomfortable and unable to break away. "Can I call you sometime?" he asked.

Suddenly Mariah jerked away. "I have to go." She jumped into her car and started the engine. Sam, still smiling a bit, watched as she pulled away. Mariah wondered why she was so phobic of dating. Sam seemed nice enough, but they definitely didn't have much in common. Maybe it was that she was afraid to start a long-term relationship with the wrong person. After all, she had dated Jack almost by default. He was there and wanted to go out with her, so she went along. At least it was fun to double date with Sandra. The familiarity that Mariah and Jack developed over the years started seeming like love—or at least a strong expectation of being together forever. She mused that being with Jack in this way might have prevented her from finding the right man for a husband. Now she was nervous about making that same mistake again.

Chapter Sixteen

At Joanne's open house, people from the neighborhood came just to look. Some realtors hovered over their clients as if they thought Mariah would try to steal them. Three couples came from the ad in the paper. One couple was interested in buying the house but said they had to wait for a certain financial source. Mariah suspected it was their parents. Another couple seemed to hit it off with Mariah and arranged to look at other houses with her during the next week. At the end of the open house, Mariah told Joanne she would be following up on the people who came by, including the agents who brought their clients.

Mariah's list of things she wanted to discuss with Alex was growing, so she headed to the park. Although Mariah's fitness had improved dramatically, the pregnancy was taking its toll on her energy level. She hiked up the hill for her little one-mile walk but turned around after about a quarter of it and headed to the flat lawn. There she sat waiting for Alex to appear. Mariah had assumed some sort of psychic energy called Alex to the park, but it didn't seem to work this time. She decided to call Alex when she got home. The call went unanswered.

Monday morning Mariah went for her walk in the park. The moment she arrived; she spotted Alex.

"Oh hi, Mariah," Alex called out. "How did things go at the open house?"

Mariah sighed. "Okay, I guess."

"Was it that bad?"

"No, actually, it was just fine. One couple came with their realtor, and I think they liked the house. Some others seemed interested but not ready to decide. I might have picked up another listing, though."

"That sounds pretty good. So why are you looking glum?"

"I don't know. I just have a lot going through my mind. And this thing has been bothering me," said Mariah, pointing at her belly.

"Your baby?"

"I can't even bring myself to call it that. It moves around and demands my attention all the time. It embarrasses me. I have a hard time thinking of it as mine. It's a constant reminder of how off the rails my life has gone."

"Well, that's a story you've made up."

"What? How can you say that? I haven't made anything up."

Mariah looked around desperately as if to find an escape, but of course, she could never outrun Alex.

"Sit down, Mariah. Let me explain a couple of things."

"Okay, start explaining." Mariah positioned herself on the bench.

"Well then, let's start with what's real. I believe it is not the actual events, but the *meaning* we make of them, that stands out in our lives. We think they are reality, but there's nothing real about them. They are just the story we made up, which we carry around as if it's reality. Take your pregnancy. It appears you are actually pregnant, but is that a cause for depression? Why aren't you excited to bring a little being into the world?"

"But I didn't ask for this! Nor did I ask for the rape that caused it."

"Didn't you once tell me that you wanted to manifest a nice job and a home with a family?"

"I guess, maybe—actually I did, but I didn't ask it to happen *this* way. And besides, family implies a mother and a father. There's no man in my life. I feel like the universe betrayed me."

"Let's take the man part. Have you done any dating?"

"Saturday night a friend of mine set me up with a blind date."

Alex laughed. "At least if he was blind, he couldn't see that you were pregnant, right?"

"That was bad, Alex. He could see me just fine. He had this way of looking at me that made me feel like he was trying to crawl into my head. And just as I feared, he walked me to my car, put his arm on my shoulder, and asked if he could call me sometime."

"And?"

"I jumped in my car and drove away."

"So, you don't want a man in your life."

"No, I mean, I don't trust men. I was abandoned by one without a word and raped by another. I'm not against having sex, just not right off the bat. I worry about every man I meet having a bad motive. I even thought that about Dick for a while. And I'm afraid of making a big mistake."

"That's another story you made up—men with ulterior motives forcing you to make a mistake."

Alex noticed that Mariah's eyes were tearing up a bit, so she spoke more gently. "Let's look at things differently. What if you were God or The Universe, as you call it, and you were trying to answer Mariah's request for a family? You sent men her way, but she always turned them away out of fear. And how would you fulfill the other part of her request for family if she rejected all men?"

"Don't say The Universe sent me a rapist!"

"Well, maybe not a rapist. Let's say an angel."

By now Mariah was yelling. "No! You've gone *way* too far!"

Alex shrugged. "The point is that it's not about you being pregnant, it's about what this means to you. The meaning is something you can change. Or not, depending on how attached you are to the meaning. Make sense?"

"I guess I'm pretty attached. Dick says I need to forgive. He says it's for my own good."

"Dick is a wise man. He helped me a lot when I was depressed. I'm sure he informed you that forgiveness was for you, right? Not for the rapist."

"But I can't see making it okay for someone to rape me. I don't want to let him off the hook."

"What hook?"

"In my mind. I need to condemn him for what he did."

"What does that do for you?"

"Ugh. It makes me feel angry that I'm a victim. It makes me unable to feel anything good about this embryo inside me. It makes me feel sad that I am stuck in this situation."

"Doesn't sound like much fun. How would you like to be feeling?"

"When I first came to Nashville, I was so excited to start all over again and manifest the life I wanted. Things were going pretty well for me, and I was looking forward to the life I thought I was going to live."

"So, Mariah, take a look at all you have going for yourself right now. You have a job. You have a decent place to live. You have a precious baby growing inside you. And now you only need to let yourself accept the right man into your life. Voilà, your vision is fulfilled. What's not to love?"

"I guess I see what you mean, but why is it so hard?"

"This might be a little too esoteric, but here goes. It's a matter of levels. When your awareness is at the level of blame and projection, you are using a part of your mind that's conditioned by this world to believe these things about condemning and holding people accountable. From that level of thinking, you would have to rationalize to forgive. That is not true forgiveness. It's more like reframing. To truly forgive, you would need to bring your awareness to a higher level that transcends the rational mind. First, you have to let go of the idea of it being about what's 'out there.' It's all about what's inside you, and I don't mean the baby. The purpose of forgiveness is to let go of the ideas and thoughts that hold you back from knowing the true love of God—or The Universe."

Mariah just sat there on the bench looking straight ahead.

Alex put her hand on Mariah's shoulder and said, "I'll be there for you any time you want to talk some more. Just call me." Then she took off for her run.

Mariah wanted to know much more, but she realized she couldn't handle it at the moment. She needed time to mull over what Alex had just said. And that would have to wait, too, because it was Monday and there was a lot to do.

Excited to work with her new buyer, Meagan, who she met handing out flyers, Mariah borrowed Dick's car to pick her up. Meagan was slightly younger than Mariah and full of exuberance for life. She had a PhD in social science and a job at Vanderbilt University. This was her first home-buying experience. Being single, she didn't need a large house but wanted to be in a professional neighborhood with a nice property. Since her listing was in one of those, Mariah knew just the right neighborhoods to show Meagan. After touring a few houses, Mariah got a sense that Meagan wanted something that had a little more pizazz. They had been looking at fairly ordinary brick houses, so they went back to the office and pored over the MLS books. It was time to increase the price range, and Meagan admitted she could easily handle a larger payment. Eventually, they found the perfect house and Mariah now felt she had a new best friend. She delivered a contract to the listing agent.

When Mariah pulled up to Dick's house to return his car, she found him working in the yard. "I have an offer out!" she shouted.

"Great! Tell me all about it."

"She's the most fun person I've ever been with. We laughed almost the whole time. I can't wait to see her again and when we close this one, I'll buy a nicer car!"

"Once you close on your listing and sell a fancy house in Belle Meade, then you'll be able to get a really nice car. Have you followed up with the other people who came to the open house?"

"Just this one I worked with today. Tomorrow I'll call the other agents who were there and also the lookie-loos."

That evening an agent called Mariah to say Meagan's offer had been accepted. Meagan was pre-approved for financing, and she had a sizable down payment ready. The sale could close within a month. Mariah was just sitting down to bask in happiness when the phone rang again. It was one of the buyers' agents who had been to the open house and had an offer to bring by. Mariah suggested they meet at her office. She drove the few blocks to the office and the agent was there within a few minutes. The offer was a good one, with only a small discount from the asking price. After the agent left, Mariah called Joanne to present it. They made an appointment to meet at eight the next morning.

The smell of freshly brewed coffee and homemade waffles wafted through the air in Joanne's house. Mariah was hungry and happily accepted Joanne's offer of a waffle with strawberry compote and a cup of coffee. Once Mariah went over the details of the offer, Joanne was in high spirits. "How long do you think it will be until closing?" she asked.

Mariah calculated the time it would take until the buyer would have financing finalized, inspections completed, and any repairs done. "Should be six weeks to two months."

"So that means we have just that much time to find the perfect home for my husband and me to move to. We'd better get started."

"I'll get right on it," Mariah replied. "I'll call you later this week with some homes for you to see."

Once Mariah got back to the office, she immediately began searching for listings in the right neighborhood and price range. Dick emerged from his office and noticed the stricken look on her face.

"What's going on? Are you all right?"

"I'm looking for houses to show Joanne now that she has a contract. I can't find a thing!"

"Of course not," said Dick. "They never list these mansions in the MLS book. The listings are handled much more discreetly. And most of them are 'pocket listings' by the agent."

"Pocket listings?"

"The agent has an exclusive listing and tries to line up a buyer himself or herself."

"Then how will I ever find a house for Joanne to buy?"

"You'll have to work your way into some very elite circles. Start with Alex. Also, ask Marla—she sometimes has pocket listings."

Mariah immediately got on the phone with Alex. "Good news, Alex. Joanne's house has a contract! I need to talk with you about what to show her. Could I meet with you today?"

"Sure, right now is just fine. Come to my house and we'll have tea."

Chapter Seventeen

Alexandria's house was amazing. The enormous mansion had perfectly manicured grounds. The stone building was old but had newer appointments throughout. Heavy wood furniture was draped with colorful throws giving the expensive dwelling a down-home feeling. They wandered through the front room to the kitchen, which was large and open. A stone fireplace stood between the kitchen and a great room on the other side. On the kitchen side, the fireplace had a hearth at about chest high with flat stones. Next to the hearth were openings in the brickwork. The left opening had wood neatly stacked. A pizza paddle and some trays for serving were on the right.

Over tea, Mariah told Alex about the sale of Joanne's house and asked if Alex had an idea of homes that might be available in her area.

"I've been waiting for you to ask. Some good friends of mine, Norman and Francesca Dearing, have already moved to California and haven't sold their house yet. They left it partially furnished to make it more attractive to a buyer. Their place is right behind us. Our backyards meet each other. I told them to wait until Joanne was ready to buy. I'm sure she'll like it."

"Great! What's the asking price?"

"We could all work together on price. My friends left me a key. I'll tell them we're ready to show your clients." Alex handed the keys to Mariah.

Mariah called Joanne to share the good news. "I'll take you to see it at noon if that works for you."

Using Dick's car again, Mariah picked up Joanne and they headed into Belle Meade to a two-story, white brick house with a round turret. Joanne was pleased right from the beginning. They toured all the rooms with Joanne making comments about what colors she would change and carpets she would pull up and replace. In the backyard, Mariah led Joanne to a grove of hickory trees and pointed out the house on the other side. "That's where Alex lives," said Mariah.

"Oh my gosh, really? I can hardly believe I could be this close to Alex."

"So, do you want to make an offer on this house?"

"Yes, I do, but first we have to show it to Frank. Can we come back later today when he's free?"

"Sure. Five o'clock?"

"I think that will work. I'll call Frank and make sure he comes home by then. I can't wait to show it to him."

Mariah headed back to the office to announce the good news to Dick.

"You're looking pretty happy today," Dick said.

"I'm actually over the moon right now. Joanne wants to make an offer on a house right behind Alex's! We're going to show it to her husband tonight. Everything is coming together and I'm going to buy a new car as soon as I get paid."

"I'm not sure you will make enough for a new car right away. I'm thinking about getting a new car, and mine is still plenty presentable. Would you like to buy mine?"

Slightly disappointed, Mariah said, "Yes, maybe."

At five o'clock Mariah, Joanne, and Frank were on their way back to the house. Frank was impressed and thought he could build some sort of a studio in the turret. They made an appointment to create an offer the next day.

Mariah arranged for Joanne and Frank to meet her at Alex's house, where Alex would get the Dearings on the speakerphone.

Dick was still at the office when Mariah returned. "Let's celebrate over dinner," he said. "How do you like all-you-can-eat fried catfish and chicken?"

"I've never had that, but I would be nervous about trying to digest that much fat. And besides, I can't eat much at a time since I got pregnant."

"Okay, then let's go to an only-as-much-as-you-feel-like-eating fried catfish and chicken place. It has a fun atmosphere and I think you'll like it."

They drove out of town to Franklin. The restaurant had an outdoor feel with string lights and tables full of guests. Mariah was pleased that the fried foods did not seem oily at all, and she found her appetite getting stronger as they ate. After dinner, Dick suggested they take a walk around the catfish pond on the lighted path that circled it.

Halfway through their walk, Mariah asked, "Do you think you are going to start dating again?"

"I'm sure I will, but first I just need to work on loving myself."

"Loving yourself?" asked Mariah. "I don't understand what you mean."

"Well, I was so in love with Shianna—infatuated, actually—that I took on everything we did and all our likes and

dislikes as my own identity. I put everything into our relationship until I don't think I even had a personal identity
anymore. That's not a bad thing, but now that she's gone,
I need to find myself again. I want to be totally delighted
with who I am before offering my romantic love to anyone
else. I need to feel whole before getting into a new relationship—and that means exploring who *I* am for a while."

As they descended some stone steps, Mariah said, "I'm
not sure how to love myself. I can't even imagine it."

"I like to think of love as just being there, all around us.
But in order to feel it, you need a way to sense it."

"What?"

"What I'm trying to say is that if love is everywhere,
how do we notice it? When you love someone or something or yourself, there is a current you can feel and that's
called emotion. Sometimes beliefs or attitudes about ourselves block the current of love energy. The more we allow
this current of love, the more we love ourselves. In fact,
any time we love anything or anyone, we are actually loving
ourselves. After all, we're the ones experiencing the feeling. When I say I'm loving myself, what I mean is that I
am opening myself to experience love in everything. It's a
feeling of joy."

"Then, are you talking about unconditional love?"

"You could say so. The biggest blockers to love are the
conditions you put on yourself."

"Then what about other emotions—anger, hate, sorrow—
those kinds of things?" asked Mariah.

"Those are all aspects of fear that come from blocked
awareness of love's presence. In actuality, there's only love."

"Well, how would I overcome those 'blockages' to experience love?"

"By loving. You have to make a practice of it until the current of love carves away the blockage."

"What should I do if I'm angry and think unloving thoughts?"

"When you pay more attention to the feelings in your body, you can start to notice how your thoughts make you feel. If you don't like the feeling you get when you're angry, then perhaps it will be easier to turn to loving. What's something you unfailingly love?"

"Um, my cat. I always love Sombra."

"Use that to get the loving started. Then hold onto the feelings you have with Sombra while you invite whatever you have anger about. Love always wins when you put it together with anything else. Remember, love is something and lack of love is nothing. When you put something with nothing, you get something, right?"

"So how does all this relate to romantic love? Somehow it seems different to me."

After a bit of silence, Dick said, "People get confused between love and need. In many cases romance is about an unspoken contract between two people that goes, 'You do that thing for me that I need in order to feel good, and I'll do that thing for you that you need.' Some people who lack the feeling of completeness crave someone to fill that need, so they think they are in love even though it actually hurts. Have you ever known anyone like that?"

"Sure, like maybe me when I was in high school."

"Okay, that should give you a good idea why I want to give myself love until I feel complete."

Dick dropped Mariah at her house. "Tomorrow, I'll help you come up with an offer price for the mansion."

Mariah wanted to ponder their conversation that night, but thoughts about her upcoming real estate transactions kept intruding. She gave up thinking and joined Sombra, who was curled up on the bed, waiting for her.

In the morning, Dick was already at the office to show Mariah some printouts of recent sales in Belle Meade. Few houses in that area went on the market, so the values were difficult to determine. They found enough to have some information to use during negotiations. Mariah asked Dick if he would go with her. Dick thought about it but assured Mariah that he trusted her to have the right instincts to do a good job.

When they finished, Mariah immediately called Joanne to set up a time when she and Frank could make an offer on the house.

"Oh, that won't be necessary," said Joanne.

"What do you mean?"

"Alex and Frank and I got together at Alex's house last night. She called the Dearings, and we all came up with an acceptable price. Norman already has an attorney working up the contract."

"Wait. What about me? Don't I get a commission on this?"

"Well, I don't see why. You brought us to the house to look at it, but that's all. Alex made all the arrangements. Besides, you are doing all the real estate stuff on our house sale, so you get the commission on that."

Mariah hung up in disbelief. In tears, she called Dick. "I can't believe it! Joanne and Alex have cut me out of the sale of the mansion!"

"Well, I don't mean to take the other side, but let's talk about what you've invested in this sale. Did you have a listing agreement in place?"

"No."

"Did you put a sign in the yard or advertise the house?"

"No."

"So, what was your part in this sale?"

"For one thing, I asked Alex if she had any ideas of a house for sale. And then I took Joanne over to see it and brought them back later so Frank could see it. Then you and I looked for houses that have sold nearby—which weren't many—to come up with a price suggestion."

"How much do you think that amount of work should be worth?"

"I didn't think about it in that way. My mind was on getting a new car," she said sheepishly.

"Measure the value of what you did to facilitate this sale against the value of your friendships and potential new contacts you will get from a good relationship with Alex and Joanne. Is it worth it to be angry?"

"I guess you're right. But it's going to be hard to forgive them for doing this."

"Your choice."

"Oh, stop. I don't feel like it's that easy."

"Start by loving yourself. Then think about how much you love them. Then decide to allow yourself to be happy and let go of your perceived slight."

"Sheesh. I feel like you just made me wrong to be angry."

"Mariah, you are making up the rules for when to be angry *and* when to think I made you wrong. The one thing you can control is your rules on how you take things."

Mariah put down the phone. She wondered why she was always the one who had to adjust. She picked up Sombra. His immediate purr calmed her. Then she tried to follow Dick's advice. She thought about how much she appreciated Alex and all that Alex had done for her. And things were going well with the sale of Joanne's house. Smiling, she decided to let go of the issue. She would do all she could to keep the good relationship she had with the two of them.

Chapter Eighteen

Mariah was eating breakfast when the phone rang. She shoved herself away from the table making sure her belly cleared the corner.

"Hello."

"Hi, it's Alex. Did I disturb anything?"

"Only the embryo. Now it's trying to do a summersault."

"I wish you would stop calling it that," said Alex. "You need to realize it's a part of you."

"It's a constant reminder of what happened to me."

"I called to offer my apology. Joanne told me she thought you were disappointed about not being part of the sale. I'm sorry for how it happened. They wanted to meet in the evening right after you showed the house to Frank, and it all just came together right away. I hope I can make it up to you in some way."

"I was disappointed at first. I guess I'm a little naive about how real estate works in places like Belle Meade. Anyway, your friendship is much more important to me than holding a grudge."

"You know the bookstore where Dick and I go? There's an ice cream shop right next door. Want to meet me there?"

"I'd love an ice cream, Alex, but it's kind of early."

"Well, it's not that early. I've already had my run."

"Okay, I haven't finished my breakfast. I'll put it away and have an ice cream instead.

They each got double scoops and sat down at a table. Mariah asked, "I remember you telling me that no matter what's going on in your life, underlying everything, you always know you have a deep pool of peace and joy. How do you get that? For me, it's just the opposite. No matter what great things are happening in my life, I still have this dark cloud of dread and fear that it's all going to fall apart."

"That must feel pretty depressing for you," said Alex. "Do you meditate at all?"

"No. I don't even know how. When I try, I just get antsy and have to stop."

"It takes practice—one of those things that has to be developed as a habit. But I can give you some pointers. Since we're right next door to the bookstore, I can show you some good books about meditation. I want to go there anyway."

They browsed together until Mariah finally decided on one of the books Alex suggested. Mariah was not absolutely convinced she wanted or needed to meditate but figured it was worth a shot. That night she went home to read the introduction hoping it would inspire her to actually want to meditate. After only a few pages, she fell asleep and didn't wake up until morning.

Meagan's new house was closing in two days. Mariah picked her up to do a final walk-through. The home inspector had required several repairs and they had to be checked before closing. To make sure the repairs had been done correctly, Mariah brought the inspection report.

Meagan was thrilled to see the house again. She was already planning where to put her furniture and what she wanted for the new patio. It was a joy seeing her dance around the house in excitement.

Finally, the closing day arrived. Mariah met Meagan at the attorney's office. A quiet tension hung in the air. There were two closing rooms, one for the buyer and one for the seller. The buyer and seller were kept separate the whole time. It seemed as if the attorney was expecting some kind of conflict to happen that could explode the whole transaction. Meagan sat confidently as if she hadn't noticed the stiffness of the environment. Mariah mused that she must be making it all up. Maybe the setting was simply official and not tense.

The closing itself went fine without any snags. At one point, Meagan asked where the property tax was split, since it was in the middle of a tax year. The attorney, who must have just finished his lunch before the closing said, "I credited it to the seller (belch) and debited it from the buyer (belch)."

Meagan and Mariah both smirked a little and stifled the temptation to laugh out loud. As soon as the closing was over, the two walked out of the building together and Meagan finally let out the laugh she had been holding. Her head started bobbing as she sang, "cred-it-ed-it, burp, burp, burp; deb-it-ed-it, burp burp." Mariah joined in as they made their way to their cars.

On the way back to the office, it occurred to Mariah that Meagan's magnetic personality indicated that she loved herself. And that love for herself allowed her to feel joy most of the time. Mariah wanted to be in that bubble of joy as much as possible. She went shopping right away for a nice housewarming gift for Meagan. The new house's windows let in a lot of light, so a plant would be a good option. Mariah also knew what colors Meagan liked from the many houses they had viewed. She chose a nice large plant with a beautiful, glazed pot. She was happy to have one more chance to see Meagan after the move.

As soon as Meagan had moved in, Mariah eagerly went to visit. Meagan loved the plant and pot and found a special place of honor for it. She was still unpacking and wondered how she had managed to accumulate so much stuff. The two laughed and chatted over a cup of tea. Finally, Mariah ventured to ask, "How do you manage to be so happy all the time? It seems like you are bubbling over with joy every time I see you."

"I've always been this way," said Meagan. "I don't know how to be *un*happy. Oh, I guess things happen sometimes that might not seem good, but I just let them pass and go on with life."

"Haven't you ever had bad things happen? Things you just couldn't let go?"

"I don't know, things like what?"

"Like being raped and then discovering you were pregnant from the rape and having to carry it."

"No, I've never had that, but I think I might just accept the individual moments rather than carrying around a continuing thought. Once I was in a car accident that killed my boyfriend. The driver of the other car was drunk, and I ended up in the hospital for a week. It took a long time to recover fully. So, the trauma of the accident was one thing. The pain and recovery were another. I took each moment as an opportunity to do whatever I needed to heal. And the nurses were so sweet! I was grateful for all their caring. And there was the loss of my boyfriend ... well, I had to take that one moment at a time, too. Eventually, the moments changed.

"I'm sorry you had to go through that. Did you want to go after the guy who hit you?"

"No, that wouldn't have done anything good for me. I'm sure the guy had to pay for what he did in some way, but I didn't spend any time thinking about it."

"Well, thanks for the tea and for talking with me. I always feel good after we've been together, and I hope we can see each other from time to time and keep a friendship going. Your positivity rubs off on me."

"You bet! I'm going to have a housewarming party soon. You'll be invited. Bring business cards and I'll be happy to introduce you to all my friends."

Mariah's feeling of lightness lasted the entire day. That evening she once again picked up the book on meditation and found it much easier to read while in her new mood. She wanted that good feeling to last forever. What was the key to Meagan's perpetually happy state? The one thing that stood out was that she simply let go of the negative thoughts and emphasized a commitment to being happy. Mariah wondered why it was so difficult for her to let go of those negative thoughts. Maybe it was just a habit. She would give meditation another try.

This time she let her awareness sink into the center of her being. A bright light expanded outward until it filled her. It felt happy. This must be what love feels like, she thought. After a few minutes, she started fidgeting and got up to move around. The feeling faded.

At the office, Dick called her to his desk. "Here's your commission check," he said. Mariah took it and awkwardly did her best impression of a happy dance.

Then Dick's broad smile faded a bit and a wrinkle appeared between his brows. "You need to have two new prospects for every sale," he said. "Have you walked or called the neighborhood around Meagan's new house?"

"No."

"Well, you can bet the seller's agent already has. Don't rest on your laurels too long. Tell all those neighbors that you have more buyers looking for houses in this neighborhood."

"But that would be a lie."

"Do you believe more buyers exist for that neighborhood?"

"Yes, of course."

"If one of those neighbors lists their house with you, don't you think those buyers will find you?"

"Probably."

"Then go get that listing."

Mariah left Dick's office feeling deflated. Why did he have to ruin my good feelings about getting a commission check?

Another closing was coming up. This time Mariah was the seller's agent for Joanne's house, so she was busier than ever and would have a hard time walking the neighborhood around Meagan's new house. She printed a few pages from the reverse directory of Meagan's new neighborhood to make phone calls that evening from home.

Joanne seemed a little tentative around Mariah who intuitively caught that Joanne needed some reconciliation over the transaction on the new house. Mariah spoke up. "I know I sounded disappointed last time we talked. I want you to know I have no hard feelings. I'm happy to be a part of the sale of your house and I hope we can have an on-going friendship."

"Oh, good," said Joanne. "I was starting to feel like I was some horrible villain to have gone behind your back."

The closing went well, and everyone seemed happy. Mariah wondered what kind of thank you gift she could give someone who now lives in a mansion.

That evening Mariah sat in meditation, but thoughts kept intruding until she gave up. Her mind was swirling around shopping for a gift, and she ended up feeling inadequate both in gift-giving and meditation. Then she remembered the call list. This put her back into a nervous turmoil over calling strangers. She had forced herself to cold call a few times, but each time it was emotionally draining. She looked at the first name and number on the list. Poised to dial, she felt a dull ache in the pit of her stomach. Calling would be awkward and go very badly.

Mariah thought back to her conversation with Dick at the restaurant. He said he needed to love himself so that he could love others. And Meagan seems to love herself. As she thought about Meagan, a soft glow seemed to form around her. Sinking into that glow, Mariah was happy and felt she could spread that happiness to anyone. She picked up the phone and began calling the list. Most of the people she called seemed genuinely glad to hear from her. Many wanted to know more details about the sale of the house and the new owner, and most of them would be perfect neighbors for Meagan. One gave Mariah the name of a person who wanted to sell her house. It was in a different neighborhood, but Mariah was happy to have the new lead.

Chapter Nineteen

Mariah felt the thud of fear taking over. She had not sensed any movement from the embryo for the last two days. *What if it's dead?* The only worse thing she could think of than carrying a rapist's baby would be carrying a rapist's dead baby. She shuddered in a cold sweat.

Mariah had not seen a doctor since discovering she was pregnant. In fact, she hadn't been proactive about anything to do with the rape or the pregnancy. Life's manifestation machinery had taken over without her in the driver's seat.

Now she knew she had to see a doctor. Still uninsured and in poverty because of her hospital bills, she returned to the county health department. Walking into the building, her old disgust of the clientele came back. She thought of them as losers and the fact that she was there made her one, too.

Finally, a woman called her into a treatment room. After what seemed like an hour, a man walked in and introduced himself as Dr. Morelli. *Just my luck they gave me a male doctor*, she thought. Without asking any questions, Dr. Morelli began taking measurements and listening with his stethoscope. "I hear a heartbeat," he announced.

Mariah's brow wrinkled so severely, it looked like her face had been wadded up. "So, the embryo is still alive."

"You sound disappointed."

"I was raped. I can't even think of this thing as mine."

The doctor went to a cabinet, pulled out a jar, and brought it over to Mariah. "You're about this far along in your pregnancy. This is what your baby looks like." Mariah was shocked. It had tiny fingers and toes. It had a face.

"You need to start thinking of it as a baby because even while it's inside, you need to be taking care of it." He let Mariah hold the jar and stare at it for a long while.

Finally, she asked, "How am I supposed to take care of it?"

"I'll prescribe some prenatal vitamins. I want you to come back in six weeks for another check-up. And watch your weight. You've already gained the recommended amount for an entire pregnancy. I can refer you to an agency if you want to give it up for adoption."

"That won't be necessary," said Mariah. Avoiding a discussion that could require a decision, she gathered up her things to leave.

On her way home, Mariah decided she could finally call it a baby. Maybe not her baby, but at least it's more of a baby than an embryo.

After the doctor's visit, thoughts of the baby kept intruding into Mariah's meditation time. As she sank into a meditative state, she could see the baby staring at her. It seemed sad. Its eyes haunted her. The baby always made her meditations depressing rather than joyful. Without being able to tap into that feeling of love and joy, it became more and more difficult for Mariah to prospect for new clients. She had none. She hadn't even called the one she got from Meagan's neighborhood.

She began dreaming about it. Sometimes the baby was angry at her and screamed at her. At other times it ran away from her, and she had to go chasing after it. She found herself talking to the baby. "You're taking away my happiness. You're going to have to stop interrupting my sleep with these ridiculous dreams."

Sometimes the baby would respond with a hard kick.

After taking the prenatal vitamins for a while, Mariah found they helped with her energy level. So, when Meagan finally called with an invitation to her housewarming, Mariah eagerly accepted it.

On the day before the housewarming, Mariah told the baby, "You had better help me get my loving back before tomorrow. No more ridiculous dreams." Just before bed, she sat to meditate with no more success. Finally, she decided to ask The Universe for help. "Dear Universe, please help me to find a way to love myself and this baby. I'm willing to give up any resistance I have that is blocking my love." Then she went to bed.

In the wee hours before daylight, Mariah had another of those dreams. This time she was walking along in a park, not unlike her favorite Percy Warner Park when she heard a cry. Curious, she went looking for its source. She came across a newborn baby under a tree. It looked pathetic. Surely it had been abandoned. Who would do this to an innocent newborn baby? Looking around, she saw no one. She picked up the poor little thing and cradled it in her arms. She began cooing and telling the baby everything would be okay. She decided to take the baby home and care for it herself. It reminded her of Chick. Whenever Mariah walked past the empty house where Chick used to live, she would feel empty, like that desire she had to cradle him in her arms and tell him things would get better had been carved out of her. Now the baby inside her needed that love and care.

Mariah woke up with an overwhelming feeling of love for the abandoned baby within her. She reached down, caressed her belly, and smiled. She could love this baby. *Her baby.* She went through the entire day with more energy than she had been able to muster all week. It felt as if she was beaming from the inside and that light shone out to everyone and everything.

She also found herself thinking about Chick more and more. Looking in the phone directory she found the number for Children's Services and called it. The woman who answered said their department was currently overwhelmed with needy children and a shortage of foster homes. She wasn't sure where Chick could be located but transferred Mariah to another department. Betty answered. She was in charge of recruiting foster families and redistributing children in overcrowded situations.

Mariah asked, "Do you know a four-year-old child named Chick who was brought to you from the police station?"

"What is the last name?"

"I don't know it. He never told me. I wonder if he even knows."

"How long ago was he brought into the system?"

"Only a few weeks."

"Okay, that narrows it down a bit. I think the last few new fosters were taken to the Clydesdale house. They had recently added bunk beds to some of the rooms, so they can stack the children up two deep. It's not an ideal situation there, but at least they have a bed to sleep in."

"Where is the Clydesdale house located? And would it be okay for me to visit?"

"The Clydesdale house is on White Bridge Road. You can look up the address in the directory. It would be best to call ahead and ask if you could visit. Fern Clydesdale could also tell you if she has Chick."

Mariah thanked Betty and hung up. She immediately looked up Fern Clydesdale and called the number. Ginny answered the call. "It's chaos here currently. You don't want to come right now. HEY! CUT THAT OUT! Mariah had to take the receiver away from her ear to recover from the loud outburst. She asked Ginny if a boy named Chick was staying there.

"Oh, Chick. I know the one you mean. Quiet one, he is. Won't even talk to anyone. He seems to be in his own world. Sure, you can come visit him, if you don't mind the noise and the mess around here."

Mariah drove to the Clydesdale house. It was an older two-story home painted white, although the paint was peeling and showed a gray color underneath. A weedy yard bracketed the concrete sidewalk, which had multiple cracks. There was a tree stump on one side of the walkway, which could have been sending roots under the concrete. That would explain the lumps in the cracked cement reaching out to trip whoever tried to reach the front door.

Mariah knocked at the door. Two children opened it and stood in the doorway. The one in front was a little girl with something smeared around her face. A slightly older boy stood behind her. He was wearing tattered, dirty clothing. His tousled brown hair obscured his eyes.

"Can I come in?" Mariah asked. The two children opened the door wider and stepped aside for Mariah to enter. "I'm here to visit with Chick. Can you show me where to find him?"

Just then Ginny approached and sternly told Mariah that she needed to check in with her or Fern before seeing a child.

"Okay, I'm Mariah. We spoke on the phone a few minutes ago. I'm here to see Chick."

"I know. I usually don't let people go back to the rooms," said Ginny. "But in Chick's case, I think it would be best if we did just that. He's so shy and quiet, he rarely comes out into all this chaos." Chick's room was in a back corner. It had a bunk bed and another twin bed indicating three children occupied the room. No one was in there. Mariah noticed a back porch at the end of the hallway. Thinking Chick probably wanted to spend his time outside, since it would have reminded him of his old home, Mariah suggested that they look for Chick back there. Once they found him, Ginny quietly left the two of them in the backyard.

"Do you remember me, Chick?"

Chick smiled and held out his left hand to show her how his cut had healed.

"I came to see how you are doing. Are things okay for you here?"

"I need to go home. I have to take care of my mom."

"Oh, honey, I'm sorry. Your mom's not there anymore."

Chick looked away. Mariah's throat constricted and her chest squeezed. How could she tell him the truth about his mother? That she was dead. Would he even know what that meant?

"Are you making friends with any of the other kids here?"

"They took my things away from me. Even if I have a stick, they take it away. They tease me."

"Is there anything I can do for you? Something you would like me to bring you?"

He wasn't looking at her anymore. He shook his head and continued to look down at the ground, so Mariah said goodbye and headed through the house to leave. On the way out, she encountered Fern holding a baby on her hip. Mariah could tell from the smell the baby seriously needed a diaper change. "Fern, are they going to be finding adoptive parents for Chick?"

"You must be joking. That kid doesn't even talk. Most people who adopt are looking for a baby, anyway, not a four-year-old."

As she drove away, Mariah wondered how she might get Chick out of this terrible situation. She couldn't adopt him. Not with a baby on the way already and no husband. Everyone she could think of was also single. Still, it hurt her to think of Chick in that house with no one who cared for him. And no one had even told him that his mother had died. A tear dripped down her cheek as she headed home.

Meagan's house was already crowded when Mariah arrived. She had to park a block and a half away, which was a good thing since she was driving her old Fiesta. Once inside the house, Meagan met her right away and began introducing her to friends, who soon exhausted Mariah's stash of business cards. One friend in particular, Betsy McGill, was interested in selling her house to buy a new, larger home. Her old house was in the same neighborhood as Mariah's. A tall slender woman with dark hair, Betsy was beautiful and imposing. She worked at Vanderbilt University and, like Meagan, was a single woman in her thirties.

"What do you do at Vanderbilt?" asked Mariah.

"I'm a senior research associate in the physics department," Betsy replied.

"Interesting. I don't know much of anything about physics, but I've seen some books recently that suggest there's a lot more to be learned about the nature of reality." Betsy was almost six feet tall and making eye contact with her was stressing Mariah's neck. She wanted to talk more and suggested they sit on some nearby chairs.

Betsy settled into the chair and said, "The nature of reality is a broad subject that's too hard to talk about in a setting like this, but I, too, have an interest in how physics applies to the way we relate to our personal lives. Perhaps we could talk more about that when you have a specific question. We'll have a chance to chat when you're showing me houses."

"That would be great. We'll want to get your house on the market right away. When would be a good day for me to measure it for a market analysis?"

"Not very soon. I want to find a house to buy before listing mine."

"I understand. Many people want to do that. But what would you do if you found a perfect house that you wanted, but couldn't get an offer accepted because you had to sell your house before you could close on the new one? Sellers aren't willing to wait for a buyer's house to sell, especially if there are any other potential buyers around. When you can offer a quick closing, most sellers are much more interested in working with you."

"I see what you mean, but how can I be sure I'll find the house I want if mine sells first?"

"You can't be sure, but what would happen if it did?"

"Oh, well, I guess I'd have to move to an apartment or something until I found what I wanted."

"That could be the scenario. Or I could bring some of our listing books so you can see how cool homes are always available at any given time."

"Thanks. Meagan was right, you are a smart real estate agent."

"Would tomorrow evening work for me to come by your house?"

"The weekend would be better. How about ten o'clock Saturday morning?"

"Perfect! I'll see you then."

Well, there we go. That's a double prospect to replace Meagan's house purchase.

She was eager to see Dick the next day to give him the news. And to talk about buying his car. As she approached the office, she saw a shiny new, metallic-blue Buick LeSabre in Dick's usual parking spot.

"How do you like it?" Dick called from his office.

"Is it yours?"

"Who else?"

"So, then, did you trade in your old car?"

"No, I didn't. I thought you might want to buy it."

"I do. That's one of the things I wanted to talk to you about."

Mariah had grown fond of the light silver Buick Regal she had been borrowing from Dick. "I don't know if I can afford it, though."

"Have you been doing your prospecting?"

"I have a new prospect from Meagan's housewarming party. She wants to sell her house and move to a larger one, and I got an idea for a potential buyer from canvassing after the sale of Meagan's house."

"Good. Then I think you should be fine with payments. Say, $200 a month?"

"I wonder if I could sell my Fiesta for anything."

"You could probably get one month's payment out of it," Dick said with a grin.

Mariah joyfully paid Dick the first payment from her commission for selling Meagan's house, and he gave her a ride in his new LeSabre to pick up the Regal. Mariah cleaned up her Fiesta right away, hoping to turn it into cash without delay.

She knocked on Arthur's door. When he opened it, she said, "I'm selling my Fiesta. It doesn't look great, but it still runs okay. Would you be interested in buying it?"

Looking away as usual, Arthur said, "No, I don't drive."

"Okay. No worries, I just thought I'd ask before I advertise it."

That night, she easily slipped into meditation. It felt good to leave behind all her daily life thoughts. Even elation over buying Dick's car and getting a great new prospect faded away.

Chapter Twenty

Betsy's neighborhood was close to Mariah's house and office. Betsy's home was only 1,200 square feet. It had wood siding and a yard that needed some upkeep. Mariah wasn't sure Betsy would get the price she was hoping for. Sitting in her car, Mariah pored through the data of recently sold homes and tapped into her feelings about giving an appropriate listing price. She sensed that she should be totally honest and let go of trying to please the client with an unrealistic amount. Knowing what appraisers look for, she decided to encourage Betsy to do some upgrading.

The yard needed a lot of help. "Betsy, do you know anyone who can do some work on the yard, or can you do it yourself? It needs to be reseeded with grass or maybe a new sod lawn, vegetation pulled away from the foundation, and some new flower beds planted in front. Also, that large lump of a shrub needs to be removed and if you added a couple of new shrubs on either side of the entrance, it would balance out the look. The buyer's first impression is important."

"I can't do it. Won't buyers just want to do the landscaping themselves?"

"A buyer would either subtract the cost to the landscape from the offer or wouldn't even be interested in looking at the house because it wasn't attractive enough. I can get a landscaper to give you a quote on it."

Betsy was starting to pout. "Maybe this was a bad idea after all. I don't want to spend a whole lot on this yard."

"I have an idea, Betsy. I know a guy who does a great job with yard maintenance around some of our rentals in this neighborhood. Why don't I have him come and give us an idea of what he could do? He might not charge as much as a professional landscaper."

"Okay, he can come take a look."

"I promised I'd show you how great houses are always available. Here are some listing books to illustrate what I am talking about."

The two women sat together on the couch and began to thumb through old listings from different seasons.

As soon as Mariah got home, enjoying her new car all the way, she immediately went to Arthur's studio to see if he could help with Betsy's yard. Arthur was hesitant at first, but Mariah pressed him to at least check it out. He could walk there, so it would not be any more difficult than some of the other rental houses he was maintaining.

When Arthur knocked on Betsy's door, she answered and showed him around the yard, explaining that she didn't want to spend much money just to sell the house. Arthur offered to do spot weeding in the lawn and prepare some flower beds. He could prune the bush in front. He suggested Betsy go to a garden store and pick out some annuals he could plant. Betsy agreed his approach sounded reasonable and gave him the go-ahead.

The next morning Arthur brought over some tools and started working on the weeding and pruning. By the afternoon, the yard already looked better. He brought some lawn seed to fill in the bare spots and places where weeds had been removed, and he reminded Betsy that the lawn needed to be watered every day until the grass seeds came up and were established. Betsy was enthusiastic enough to go out and buy some annuals for the beds.

In contrast, Mariah felt depressed. Getting the listing with Betsy seemed more complicated than she had originally thought. She tried to love herself, but it went nowhere. Meditation seemed impossible again, and she had forgotten to use any of her other tools. She needed Alex.

"Why is it so hard to keep up with meditating and loving myself or even with gratitude?" Mariah asked Alex at the park.

"People seem to cling to their pain as if it defines them, I guess. They get attached to those negative feelings and it's addictive. Letting go of the beliefs, thoughts, and memories feels like losing one's identity. Does that resonate with you?"

"Well, sort of. But I don't think I can deny reality. If I walk around all happy as if none of these problems exist, I'm not being real with myself."

"Reality is totally subjective. Your reality is different from mine or anyone else's. Another total reality exists, where those individual . . . I'll call them limitations . . . don't exist. That's where forgiveness comes in. All the problems you can imagine are just limited thinking that needs to be forgiven. Forgiveness is releasing the beliefs and thoughts that make a person suffer. Isn't that what you want, ultimately?"

"You know that forgiveness is impossible for me. I can't just let go of the rapist who did this to me—or my old boyfriend Jack, for that matter. In my mind, I wish there was some way I could punish them and make them suffer as much as they made me suffer."

Alex lay back in the grass with her arms under her head. "I've noticed that as a general rule, everyone unconsciously wants oneness. They want others to feel what they are feeling to have that connectedness. The trouble comes when they want others to connect with them at the level of their pain. We all carry beliefs in the physical and mental realm, but we also still have the realms of love and non-judgment within us. The more we keep our mind occupied at the level of pain, we forget that love and non-judgment exist. Until we're able to forgive the pain, letting it go, it will be difficult to experience oneness at the love level. Make sense?"

"So, are you telling me I want a connection with the rapist so that he can feel the pain he has inflicted upon me? Hmmm. I guess I do want him to know what he did to me. And not from just being told. I want him to feel my pain until he is really sorry. I wish I could twist the knife a bit to make him feel even worse."

"And that would make you feel better?"

"Somehow, I think it would. No. I wanted it to cancel out all the bad feelings he had caused me so that they would just disappear. Gone forever. But that's probably not how it would work."

"Right. At least you're beginning to get what you *do* want to feel. That's progress, isn't it?"

Mariah wanted to talk to Betsy again about the physics they had discussed at Meagan's housewarming. And she needed to get the listing. She met Betsy at her house after work. Betsy was thrilled with the improvements Arthur made to the yard and was in a better mood about listing the property. Once they signed the listing paperwork, Mariah asked, "Remember when we talked about physics and reality at Meagan's? I'd like to learn more of your thoughts on that."

"Well, physics encompasses an enormous amount of inquiry, from the objects we see in the universe to tiny subatomic particles. What we do in physics is measure things. That's about it. But what we learn from measuring things has an enormous impact on what we see and understand about our world.

"My research is on the subatomic level, and you might think that would have nothing to do with how we see our daily lives. But it has taught me a lot about how much space there is in everything. Do you have a concept of how much space there is between the sun and the planets?"

"Vaguely."

"So, take that idea of space and apply it to the tiniest molecule. Within that molecule, there are particles that make it up. And those particles are as far apart as the sun and its planets, relatively speaking. And the space between each atom making up a molecule is like looking out into space to the next stars, again relatively speaking. Much more space than mass exists in what we *think* is solid. Get it?"

"How does this fit into the physical world?"

"Indirectly. I have a friend who is a neurophysiologist. He told me something about perception—and it's fascinating. To make any sense of this jumble of space-filled atoms, we've developed sensory organs to see, feel, and hear at a specific level. And what we think we see is only a tiny part of what is out there all around us. That's because our brains can't process everything all at once, so we just focus on certain things and let everything else pass by unnoticed. Then our brains fill in details—that may not have even been there—to sense the flow of reality."

"Are you saying we are making a lot of it up?"

"In a way. Our brain wants everything to fit into its idea of reality. Have you ever stared at a wall and then started to see faces in its little bumps and crevices?"

"I have, actually."

"Your brain wants to recognize patterns. It also wants everything to make sense based on learned beliefs and cultural agreement. Part of that perception is just about the limitations of our sensory apparatus. As a physicist, I know that we can only measure what we have instrumentation to detect. And then we have subconscious beliefs that further limit what we can perceive. I read about a man who was part of a perception experiment. The researchers strapped him to a chair and proceeded to heat a branding iron right in front of him until it was red hot. They took the branding iron around behind him and immediately put ice on his back. The man screamed in pain and red welts formed on his back as if he had been burned. There are numerous reports of other experiments like that, which shows that reality isn't an absolute thing, and what a person experiences depends quite a lot on their programming and expectations."

"Whew! My mind is swirling," said Mariah. "I'd better give this some time to sink in. Thank you for sharing it with me." She stood to leave. "I'll have a for sale sign put in your yard this week and start advertising."

The next morning, Mariah charged into the office to start on the listing. Humming to herself, she began writing the ad copy and flyer. She called the photographer and the sign guy. Soon the phone started ringing with general office business and Mariah was glad to have gotten a head start on the listing before getting bogged down.

Later in the afternoon, a woman walked into the office and told Mariah she was there to see Dick Hansen. She wore a glitzy, sequined dress accessorized with too much jewelry. *Trying to be a magazine model*, thought Mariah as she noticed the woman's blonde hair with dark roots and her uneven and too-thick makeup. Dick came out of his office and introduced her as Patsy. He wanted to show her his real estate business before they went out to dinner and a concert. Mariah couldn't believe it. *Surely Dick had better taste than that!* She hoped he wasn't blinded by Patsy's fake glitz. Mariah had always thought of Dick as a down-to-earth kind of man who would value naturalness.

Walking home, Mariah couldn't get it out of her mind. *What could Dick see in this woman who clearly looked like she was trying to be something she was not?* Maybe she didn't know Dick that well after all.

Eager to talk to Alex again, Mariah went to the park the next morning about the time she thought Alex would be there. Sure enough, Alex was just cooling down from her run.

"My new client messed my mind about reality," said Mariah.

"Good!" replied Alex. "Maybe that will knock you out of your stubborn grip on what you think is real."

"Why did you say that? Don't I have a right to hold on to my reality?"

"Sure, you do, and you have a right to the emotional state it puts you in, as well."

"Okay, let's say I'm ready to loosen the grip on my reality. Where does that leave me?"

"It gives you some freedom to experience life as you want. Just allow what you've learned about reality—that it is not fixed—to reveal possibilities you didn't know before. That's all."

Mariah heaved a big sigh. "All right. Betsy said that our minds don't take in everything that happens around us and that we fill in the spaces between our experiences with whatever makes sense. The experience that bothers me most is the rape and its result," she said pointing at her belly. "I can't see how I made that up."

"What did you actually experience when you were raped?"

"I was walking to my car at night when a man wrapped his arms around me and knocked me down to the sidewalk. My head hit the sidewalk so hard I passed out and didn't wake up until days later in the hospital."

"How did you know it was a man?"

"He was heavy."

"Okay, someone heavy wrapped you up and knocked you to the ground. Do you know you were knocked to the ground? Or could you have stumbled on your own?"

"Geez, I don't know. I was wearing these horrible high heels, and one heel lost its tap, so I was unsteady, but I know this man grabbed me and I fell forward."

"All right, you were grabbed by someone heavy while you were unstable in high heels, and you fell forward on the sidewalk and were knocked unconscious. Is that about right?"

"Wow. That sounds so empty. Are you saying that what makes it seem so powerful is the story I've made around it?"

"You know, what I like about you, Mariah, is how quickly you pick up things like this. You're a good student of life!"

"Still, here I am pregnant. That means it was a man and he raped me."

"Can you absolutely know it happened at the same time?"

"How can it be anything else?"

"Well, Mariah, if I told you, then I would just be making up a new story, but here goes . . . you said you were unconscious for a few days. Can you rule out the rape didn't happen sometime later by someone else, either on the sidewalk or at the hospital?"

"No, I can't rule that out, but it's unlikely."

"Right. But the point of this inquiry is to arrive at a state of 'I don't know.'"

"Yes! I don't know! Then what? I'm still angry that this happened. I'm angry at The Universe. I've been robbed of so much."

"Do you remember I once said that what you feel was taken away from you is the thing you need to give yourself? Think about that for a while until you know how to give yourself what you feel was stolen. And don't forget to ask for help from your spiritual guides during your meditation."

Mariah was silent and leaned on her forearms against her thighs. "What would I ask my guides for?"

"You don't need to be too specific. Give your guides the latitude to communicate in a myriad of channels."

"Thanks, Alex. I'll give this a try."

Chapter Twenty-One

What was lost? The question rattled around Mariah's head in a monotonous cycle. It seemed the answer, whatever it was, was nebulous and undefined. It would have been so much easier if she had lost a thing or a bag of money or something; but no, it was deeper and more hidden than that.

She decided to start a list.

She wrote:

MY HAPPINESS.

How could that happen? How could another person take away my happiness? Well, it had happened. Okay, but there must be something else to it.

MY FUTURE.

He forced a future on me that I didn't choose.

CHOICE. That's it. I didn't choose to be pregnant now. And he'd forced me to lose my job. He made me feel violated. That means I'd lost something. What was it?

MY SELF IMAGE.

My idea of being in charge of manifesting my life. I felt embarrassed. Like I'd made some terrible mistake. Unwed mothers are stupid to get pregnant, so that makes me stupid, too.

Now Mariah looked at the list. How could she give these things to herself? Well, to be honest, she'd had many more episodes of happiness since learning how thoughts affect feelings. At least she now had some tools to make it easier to be happy. Score one for that, anyway.

But what about choice regarding her future? Wasn't that taken away? What had she chosen for her future? She remembered coming to Nashville with a plan to manifest a nice home with a great job and a family. Family was most important.

With a clearer picture of what she wanted, Mariah grabbed her pen and began to write again:

A NICE HOME.

Well, my house isn't half bad. Thanks to Arthur, it's beautiful outside. And I have the freedom to do whatever I want with it on the inside.

A GREAT JOB.

To be honest, I like my job at the realty a lot better than the job at the attorney's office. I have easier hours and the option to get a much higher income selling houses.

A FAMILY.

That's a trickier one. True, being pregnant means children will come sooner rather than later, but what about a husband? That's not something I could give myself, is it? Okay, maybe I could be more open to meeting men. But what man would want to date a woman who is already pregnant?

SELF IMAGE.

I know I could do better at that. "I think unwed mothers are stupid" is something I could work on changing. Where did I even get that idea, anyway? But how could I get over my mistrust of men?

Looking at her original manifestation goals made Mariah eager to work on the items she felt she had lost after the rape. She needed to see herself differently by forgiving her attitude about unwed mothers. Then she could get down to inviting the right man into her family. *Her family.* That was the first time Mariah had thought about the baby she was carrying and herself as a family. Mariah was eager to talk this over with Alex.

As she walked out her front door, her senses were overcome with the vibrant beauty of what was before her. The dark green foliage contrasted with purple blossoms accented with yellow and orange daisy-like flowers. If she could eat beauty like this, she would have gorged herself until she lay in a stupor. Instead, she walked to work.

Mariah urgently needed to find a buyer for Betsy's house because Betsy was impatient to find her future home. Mariah had made an appointment with Betsy to look at houses on Sunday to narrow it down a bit. Mariah advised Betsy that if she saw any houses on her own she wanted to look at, she should call Mariah, not the listing agent, about it.

On Saturday, Mariah tried to meet Alex but didn't find her in the park. She took her walk and wondered if that was smart since she'd be walking a lot later. After freshening up, Mariah grabbed a stack of flyers and followed through on her plan to walk Betsy's neighborhood to see if she could scare up a potential buyer. Perhaps a renter or someone with a smaller home would be interested.

It was already eighty degrees, which made the task of canvassing more difficult. Thankfully, many homeowners invited her to talk inside their air-conditioned houses. As the day wore on, Mariah forged ahead even though the oppressive humidity felt like walking through hot molasses. Her hair stuck to her face and neck with sweat and her shirt clung to her skin. At least her bedraggled appearance encouraged more people to ask her inside.

At one of the houses, the occupants invited Mariah in. They introduced themselves as Ann and Willard Nelson. They were renters but wanted their own home. Mariah qualified their income to make sure she could offer them some help. They would need at least $5,000 for a down payment but could qualify for a house in their same neighborhood. Between their savings and an extra car, they could sell, this made purchasing a house seem doable. Mariah wanted to show them Betsy's home right away. She called Betsy first and then brought the Nelsons over. The young couple was excited to be looking at a place they could potentially own. They wanted to make an offer right away, but Mariah counseled them to get pre-qualified for a loan and sell their car to know they were on firm footing. And she referred them to a mortgage broker who would be happy to work with them.

As soon as she got home, Mariah called Alex, saying she'd like to continue their conversation.

"Come on over, Mariah," Alex quickly responded.

As Mariah drove to Alex's house, the clouds grew darker, and the humidity became stifling. By the time she arrived, lightning danced in the distance and appeared to be moving toward them.

"I've been thinking about what I had lost. I even wrote a list," said Mariah.

"Oh, smart girl! Let's have a look."

"Well, it's just a sketch. I can see how most of it is being regained or is not an issue for me now. But the self-image thing, well, I don't know how to overcome it. And then there's the husband part."

"Let's deal with this belief about unwed mothers here," Alex said, looking at Mariah's notes. "Do you see any benefit from holding on to that belief?"

"No, none at all. But I don't know how to change it."

"When you see someone else who is an unwed mother, do you always think they are stupid?"

"Yes, I do. During high school, my parents always drummed into me to resist the temptation to have pre-marital sex. They made sure I understood that boys would sometimes try to pressure me to have sex and that I should stand up to them and not be stupid enough to get pregnant. A few girls in my school did get pregnant, and I saw how miserable their lives were."

"I'm glad you were able to see so clearly the origin of that belief. Knowing your disempowering beliefs is the hardest part for some people. Can you forgive those girls?"

"Yes, I suppose so. It didn't affect me, and besides, every-one makes mistakes."

"And did you even make a mistake?"

"No! I didn't even make a mistake. I was a victim."

"Who decided you were a victim?"

"Oh. I did."

"Good," said Alex. "That was to give you the motivation to let this belief go. Now you've done all the mental work. The next part requires a higher power."

At that point, a giant peal of thunder shook the house and both women laughed.

"What do you mean, higher power?" Mariah asked, her belly still heaving with laughter.

"Do you pray, Mariah?"

"I'm not sure how to answer that. I've been trying to meditate. Sometimes it works to get into a better state."

"That's a start. Do you remember me telling you to imagine your higher self, or maybe a guardian angel trying to help you get the life you ask for?"

"Oh, you mean like the one that brought me a rapist to make a baby?"

"You make it sound like your higher self is your enemy. Think of it like this: Your higher self is part of you. It has one foot in heaven, but still has a connection with you here in this physical world. It's like a translator to The Universe, as you call it. The purpose of prayer is to be in communication with your higher self and The Universe. So, step into being your higher self if you can. Imagine *you* are trying to give *yourself* the life you want. What do you do?"

"I don't know. I guess I would need more information—about the life I want."

"Exactly. Get yourself into a meditative state where communication with your higher self is more possible. Then ask for help letting go of this disempowering belief about unwed mothers. It works for all kinds of forgiveness. The purpose of thinking it through is to open up a *willingness* for the forgiveness to take place."

"I see. So, I don't have to do it myself, I can turn it over to my higher self?"

"Exactly. And once you turn it over, don't overthink it or take it back. You have to let go of it. Thinking it through like we did earlier is just to build your willingness to let it go."

"Wow."

"Let's deal with the man thing. Now that you know what is missing from your dream family, you can build up the desire to forgive men and allow that part of your dream to manifest."

"I still don't feel ready for that kind of forgiveness."

"That's what I'm talking about. You get to use your reasoning power to build up the desire. What are the attributes you would want in a man?"

Mariah put her head in her hands. "I don't know what I want in a man. I just don't think I can trust anyone right now."

"Then you want someone you can trust, right? What else?"

"Okay, I want a man who will respect me. Someone who cares about my ideas and who communicates well. Also, a man who likes to be physically affectionate, like hugging and holding hands. More like best friends forever. I want a life partner."

"Nice. You're getting the hang of this. What else?"

"A good father. I want a great family man who wants to share the responsibility and activities of being in a family. That's the most important."

"Write all this down. You're doing great. Have you ever thought about these things before?"

"No, not really. I think I saw it in pictures in my mind but never put it down like this," said Mariah as she wrote her list.

"As you think about these attributes, how do you feel about finding him?"

"Charged up. But where would I look for someone like that?"

"You don't have to know that. Just keep being who you are. The point of a list is to help you recognize the right one. When you want a man with these attributes strongly enough, you'll be willing to do your forgiveness."

"You would say that," grumbled Mariah. "You know, it occurs to me that most of the ways people go about meeting someone—like going to bars—are pretty bad at bringing people together for marriage. The problem is that I don't do much of anything else where single men would be hanging out. When I go to the park, I see almost all couples. And you."

"When you are clear about what you want and who you are, it creates a certain magnetism, which works in two ways. As you're probably hoping, it attracts your desires toward you. But it also draws you to a path that brings you closer to your dreams. They work together. If you are true to yourself and stay focused on what you want to attract, it will feel like you are doing nothing, and people and things come easily. You can relax. On the other hand, if you go to bars looking for a man who wants to stay home with a family, it means you have strayed off your true path, see?"

The thunder had abated, although it was still pouring rain. Mariah left Alex's house and carefully drove home. The pavement was shiny, and the reflected streetlights made it difficult for Mariah to stay in her lane. She was relieved when she finally arrived home and grabbed Sombra for some cuddles.

Just before going to bed, Mariah sat down for her meditation. She slipped into a meditative state easily, as if she was just allowing it to happen. Then she asked to communicate with her higher self. She noticed her head gently rocking forward and back as if to be nodding yes. Then she asked her higher self to relieve her of the belief that unwed mothers are stupid. After that, she merely sat in awareness of her willingness to let it go. Then she thanked her higher self and went to bed.

The next morning, she tested her thoughts. "Unwed mothers are stupid" did not resonate at all. It was a dead thought. Mariah felt happy. Apparently, her unborn baby felt that way, too, as it did a full somersault.

What she was learning about making lists helped her sort out all kinds of things. She was eager to use it to help Betsy get clear on what kind of house she wanted. So, before going to look at houses, Mariah asked Betsy to describe what she wanted in a new home. "How do you see yourself living in it?"

"Well, it's bigger than this one and nicer, too."

"Do you see yourself doing some gardening?"

"No. I can't seem to keep up with all that."

"So maybe a condominium or zero lot line would be a good fit."

"I don't want a condominium. It would seem more like an apartment. I want a separate house, so it feels like I'm a homeowner."

"Okay, I think we can find some homes with small yards, or maybe a development with lots of open space maintained by a homeowner's association. What would you like to be doing inside this house?"

"I like to cook. Brunches are my favorite. I hope to have friends over for brunches or dinners."

"Perfect! So, a big kitchen might be important. And maybe open to a great room so you can talk with your guests while you cook?"

"Yes! That's it."

"And how do you see yourself in the house when you're not entertaining?"

"I hope to find someone to share it with. Someone I can snuggle up with to watch a movie. And she would like to cook, too. We could have breakfast together every day. Hey, thanks for getting me to flesh that out. I can see it much more vividly now."

The day went well, with Mariah showing Betsy the type of place she might want to buy. Without all that information, Mariah would have never found the right houses to show.

Chapter Twenty-Two

Mariah was sick. She had been awake most of the night. Fever dreams drifted through awareness of throbbing pain in her head and fire in her throat. She pulled herself up from bed and tried to go to the kitchen for water. Halfway through, she became so dizzy she had to grab the bedroom door frame. Turning around, she tried to crawl into bed but fell to the floor. Her second attempt was successful, but now she was back in bed without water. She lay there, tears in her eyes, feeling helpless.

Several hours later she tried again to get to the kitchen. This time she made it to the sink and filled her glass. She was unable to swallow, however. It was almost time to go to work, so she dialed the office. The answering machine picked up and she tried to speak. In a grunting croak, she uttered, "I'm sick . . . can't come in." Then she went back to bed and pulled the blanket over her head.

A while later she heard the phone ring but couldn't make herself get up to answer. It rang again. And again.

When Dick got her message, he figured Mariah must be terribly sick since she didn't answer any of his calls and decided to go check on her. On the way, he stopped by a little market to pick up a few things he thought she might need—a thermometer, some electrolytes, Jell-O, cups of pudding, and a can of soup with a light broth.

Not wanting to knock and force her to get up, he used his rental key to let himself in. From the front room, he called, "Mariah, it's Dick. Are you all right?" There was no answer. He set the groceries down in the kitchen. "Are you all right?" Still no answer, so he approached her open bedroom door and stuck his head just inside the room. There she lay with her mouth opening and closing without sound.

Her eyes were puffy, and her neck was enlarged. Dick came over to her bed and put his ear close to her face and heard a whisper.

"I can't swallow. Even my saliva won't go down," she said showing him a wet towel.

Dick pulled the thermometer from its box and put it into her mouth. It beeped at 103. "You need to go to the emergency room."

"No," she whispered. "Can't afford."

"Who is your doctor?"

Mariah shrugged.

"You must have *some* doctor. Who is your OBGYN?"

Another shrug.

Dick left the room and dialed his own doctor. He left a message with the office staff for the doctor to call him and gave them Mariah's number. Dick's doctor had been with the family since Dick was a child. Back then, the doctor would make some house calls. Dick wasn't sure if things had changed. Dr. Schwartz called back shortly, and Dick explained Mariah's predicament. The doctor said he didn't normally make house calls anymore but would come by after he was finished with his appointments around six-thirty. Dick sighed. That's at least seven hours, he thought.

In the meantime, Dick wrang out wet cloths and placed them on her forehead to try to get the fever down. His attempts to get Mariah to take little sips of water were a lost cause, as most of it still came back out on the towel.

Wandering through the house Dick noticed the spare bedroom had nothing to make it resemble a nursery. Mariah wasn't at all ready for what was to come in approximately six weeks.

Dr. Schwartz arrived at six twenty-three, a few minutes earlier than expected. He took Mariah's temperature and looked at her throat. "You have strep throat," he said. "I'm going to give you an antibiotic shot." When he finished, he turned to Dick and said, "Call me if she doesn't get better soon."

Shortly after her shot, Mariah fell asleep, and Dick decided he could go home. The next morning, he wanted to check on Mariah but was afraid he was invading her space too much. A phone call might not work if she still couldn't speak, and she would have to get out of bed and walk to the kitchen to answer. He finally decided to go in person after all. He knocked on her door, then unlocked it. Opening it slightly, he called out.

"I'm here," said Mariah softly, but with more volume than the night before.

Dick understood that "here" meant her bedroom, but he only stepped into the living room. "How are you doing?"

"Lots better! The shot last night helped almost immediately. I still feel sick, but I'm sure I'll be able to come back to work soon."

"No need to worry about that. Is there anything you'd like me to take care of with your contracts?"

"I don't think so."

"I'd be happy to bring you something to eat. I can heat some soup."

"No, please! I am embarrassed about you coming here to take care of me. You're my boss, and it just feels strange for you to be here."

"Okay, I'm leaving now. Drink lots of water. And, honestly, Mariah, you have to get a doctor—someone to handle the birth of your baby."

After returning to the office, Dick sat at his desk pondering his relationship with Mariah. He was concerned about her. She didn't have a doctor to deliver her baby. She didn't even have anything ready in her house for a baby. It was as if she still didn't believe it was going to happen. He longed for a deeper connection with Mariah, who had been his communication link when he was home with Shianna. Mariah was so easy to talk to, and he wanted to help her in any way he could. He hoped his attempt to help her when she was sick wouldn't ruin the relationship they had built up.

When Mariah came back to work a day later, Dick asked her to come into his office and he shut the door behind them.

"Mariah, first I want to apologize for imposing myself on you when you were sick. One thing I've learned about myself is that I'm a nurturer. While Shianna was bedfast, I got good at it. Now I've started volunteering at the hospital where Alex works, helping the nurses change sheets, move patients, and sometimes bathe them. That's why it seemed natural for me to want to help you when you were sick. I just didn't realize it would embarrass you so much."

"That's okay. I just want to keep our working relationship clean. You know what I mean?"

"Sure."

The next time he was volunteering, Dick ran into Alex. He asked her to meet him in the cafeteria for a coffee when their shifts were over.

"Alex, I wonder if I could ask for your help with a mutual friend."

"No problem. Who is it?"

"It's Mariah. She's due to have her baby in about a month and a half, and she's done nothing to prepare.

"Wow. I guess she's still in denial. What can I do?"

"I was thinking about giving her a baby shower. I can't get involved with that because she wants to keep me out of her personal life, since I'm her boss. I could help you with the guest list, though. I know all her clients, and I'm also familiar with her former coworkers. I'd give you their names and addresses if you could plan it."

"That's a fun idea! I love those personal gatherings. Baby showers are my favorite! Would we do it at her house? Best not a surprise."

"I'm going to leave that to you. I really can't be involved with anything besides the guest list. And do *not* tell her I suggested it."

"Okay, I won't even call her. It's pretty easy to just happen to run into her in the park."

It took two days before Alex finally saw Mariah at the park, sitting on a bench looking straight ahead, deep in thought.

"Hi, Mariah, how are you doing?"

Startled, Mariah blurted, "Terrible!"

"Ouch. What's the problem, now?"

"My life, that's the problem."

"That's a pretty broad statement."

"I just look at my life and it sucks. I don't know how to change it."

"Specifically?"

"Okay, how about an unwed mother unprepared to give birth, much less bring home a baby, with no one to help?"

"Do you *want* to keep this baby and get prepared? If not, you could check out adoption services."

"I guess I want to keep it, but it just seems so hard to get ready. And I don't have a doctor for delivery, either."

"I know a midwife I could refer you to. If she's available, she could assist with the delivery, and she can transfer you to the hospital if there's any problem."

"That would be good."

Alex raised her eyebrows in puzzlement, "Are you having a baby shower?"

"No. Anyway, I don't have that many friends."

"I think you'd be surprised. Usually, a friend plans the shower for you. Would you mind if I did that?"

"Wow, would you?"

"Of course, I would. You could give me a list of your friends and I'll invite them. Or I could ask Dick."

"No! Don't ask Dick. He came to my house when I was sick. I was so embarrassed! He even came into my bedroom, took my temperature, and called his doctor. He kept trying to get me to drink water, which I couldn't swallow. And I was too weak to do anything about it."

"Dick is such a nurturer, isn't he? He's so gentle and caring, and it gives him so much joy to give in this way."

"Joy ... so that's how he gets it?"

"Giving to others is one of the best ways to get joy. It doesn't even require you to start out liking it. Just doing it brings joy automatically. You should try it."

Mariah turned away. "I don't think there's anything I can give."

"Didn't I hear you're great with math?"

"I guess. I check contracts and help other agents with recommendations for financing."

"Well, that's giving! Plus, I have an idea for a volunteer opportunity if you're willing to look into it."

"What is it?"

"A high school has a summer program for girls who are trying to graduate while they're pregnant. One of the girls needs a math tutor. Could you help her out?"

"I guess. I'd probably fit right in with the unwed mothers."

"Meet me at Hillsboro High School tomorrow afternoon at four o'clock, and I'll introduce you to her counselor."

"Okay, I will, although I can't imagine it'll give me joy."

The next day, Mariah and Alex were in Mrs. Bates's office. Alex explained that Mariah was good with math and would be willing to tutor Ramona. Alex would serve as the character reference. Ms. Bates had Mariah fill out a form and then walked her down the hall to a room with five pregnant girls, all independently studying. She called Ramona out to the hall and introduced her to Mariah. Ramona's eyes immediately went down to Mariah's belly.

"You're pregnant too?"

"I sure am. I'm due in August, how about you?"

"About the same, I guess."

Mariah asked Ms. Bates, "Where can we go to study math?"

"Just use the back of this same room. You shouldn't need to talk too loudly. You'll only have about an hour before we have to close up the building until tomorrow."

Mariah was able to help Ramona right away with some difficult story problems. "Here's what you do. Break the problem down and determine exactly what you need to know from each part and then put them together to solve the problem. Don't get stuck on irrelevant details like people's relationships."

Before they had to leave, Ramona asked Mariah for more details about her pregnancy. Mariah answered openly about the circumstances of her pregnancy and her struggles with it.

Ramona looked down, tears welling in her eyes, "I feel so stupid right now. I can't believe I got myself into this situation. I was in love, I guess. My boyfriend was so insistent about sex, and I thought we were going to get married as soon as he graduated. But when he did, he left town for college. His parents told him to break up with me, and my parents kicked me out of our house. I'm sleeping on my friend's couch now."

"I'm so sorry," said Mariah. "I know how rough it is. The only thing you can do is make the best of the present situation and look ahead to making some new positive choices. And I don't think you're stupid. You just made a mistake."

"Thanks, Mariah. You've helped me a lot. Thanks for the math help and also for just being here and listening to me. I needed someone to listen without judgment. You are great!"

That brought tears to Mariah's eyes, as they hugged and said goodbye for the evening. Mariah left with a big smile. All the way home she felt—*joy*!

Chapter Twenty-Three

Dick dropped by Mariah's desk just before her time to leave. "Some of us are going fishing tomorrow. Want to come along?"

"I'd love to but I don't have any fishing gear right now," Mariah replied with an exaggerated sad face.

"You do like to go out in the woods, though, right? Come with us to just hike around and you can eat some of what we catch."

"Who else is going?"

"Mark is going, and I think Roxanne and her husband, George also."

Mariah tried to imagine a human Barbie doll in fishing gear. "I might try to come along. I probably need a break from real estate for a day."

"That's the spirit!"

Mariah had not worn her jeans for months. She pulled them on just to see if she could fashion a way to keep them up unzipped. They wouldn't even go over her hips. Resigned to just wearing her everyday stretch-panel slacks, she paired a long t-shirt with them and figured she could put on the colorful striped Converse sneakers if her swollen feet would fit. It was tight but would have to do. She found enough bread and some peanut butter for a sandwich in the refrigerator, and she had peaches. Peaches had become Mariah's craving the last few weeks.

Mark and Dick were loading the back of Mark's old Jeep Cherokee at the office. Roxanne introduced Mariah to her husband, George. They were planning to follow along in their own vehicle, although Dick had hinted the drive might add extra wear and tear on their little Cadillac Cimarron. Mariah had only a duffel bag with her lunch, a pan, a hunting knife, and matches. She intended to forage while the others fished.

They drove past Hendersonville, and then onto a smaller paved road that ran along a river. Mariah wasn't sure what river it was. She didn't see a sign for it, even when they had crossed over a bridge. Looking back, Mariah could see Roxanne and George right behind them. "Is this the river we're going to fish?" Mariah asked.

Mark laughed. "Yes, but way upriver from here. I know a guy who owns property up there. It's up a dirt road. We'll be turning onto it in a few miles."

When they did, the gravel road began climbing more steeply before leveling off. The ride was bouncy in the Jeep. Mariah could only imagine what Roxanne and George were thinking. Finally, the road began to wind back down toward the creek. They reached a spot that looked like a dead end. Mark turned off the engine and hopped out. "Here we are."

George parked right behind Mark, got out, and wiped his brow. "That last part was harrowing," he said. "I hope I can find a way to turn around when it's time to leave."

Everyone except Mariah got out their fishing gear. Roxanne was outfitted with a full ensemble for fly fishing. She was already wearing a vest with some flies attached to a patch. High boots with felt soles hung from the back of her vest. Her pole was still in a tube with a zipper at the top. With a dashing fisherman's hat, she looked like an advertisement in a slick outdoors magazine. George wore a matching outfit. They were so excited, it was contagious.

Mark stood in front of the whole group to orient everyone. "The creek is pretty good for trout from here upstream. Downstream a way is a deeper, wider area. It's kind of marshy on the banks, but you can catch bass and catfish there. I'm going downstream for some bass."

Dick and Mark headed downstream while Roxanne and George prepared their fly poles and reels for upstream trout fishing. Mariah looked around and decided to head into the woods to forage.

The forest was buzzing with annual cicadas. As she climbed back up the embankment toward the woods, a black swallowtail butterfly flew over her shoulder and fluttered into the brushy forest. She followed it to an area thick with brush. Two more swallowtails appeared, and Mariah pushed her way into the spot where they landed. *Spicebush*, she thought. As she looked more closely, she could see some small berries, a few of which were turning red. Recognizing the plant, she popped a few berries into her mouth. Their intense flavor was unmistakable. She lifted the bottom of her t-shirt and began picking a good handful. As she pushed her way out of the spicebush thicket, she found some lamb's quarters and a rose bush with petals to add to the collection. If they catch some fish, she thought perhaps something lemony would be useful. Mariah began searching the ground for wood sorrel. That brought her into an area with some pine trees where she found not only wood sorrel but also some old pine limbs with knobs of hardened pitch. She could use these to start a fire. Blackberries and raspberries grew along the ground, but very few were ripe.

Returning to the creek, Mariah found a large flat rock and unloaded her stash of goodies. She sat on another rock and ate her sandwich and peach. The midday sun was getting hot, so as soon as she finished her lunch, she rolled up her pants and waded into the creek. The cold fresh spring water stung at first, but once her feet became accustomed to it, she noticed the soft feeling of round moss-covered stones. She waded a little deeper and saw small fish about the size of her finger swimming around her. Nibbling her legs. Mariah looked up to see Roxanne and George wading back toward her. "Hey, catch anything?"

"Lots ... of branches," laughed Roxanne. "We're tired already. If we can figure out how to turn the car around, we're going to head home. Will you tell Dick and Mark?"

"Sure, no problem, but don't you want to wait and see if they catch some fish?"

George turned to Mariah and said, "I saw a fish restaurant on the way up. We'll just have our lunch there."

Resuming wading, Mariah noticed something move near her feet and disappear under a larger stone. Crawdads? She started picking up rocks, one by one until a good-sized crawdad darted out. Thinking she could put them in her duffel bag, she waded back to the shore and grabbed it. The duffel was empty except for the pan, hunting knife, and matches. She set those things next to the herbs and berries and sloshed back into the stream. The sun reflecting off the water made seeing the stones on the bottom difficult, so she decided to cross the creek to the shadier side. As she did so, the water got deeper and she slipped and fell, floating a good four or five feet before she could get herself upright. Mariah laughed. At least she didn't have to worry about getting wet, now. In the shade, she was able to see the creek bottom. There were plenty of big rocks for craw-dads to hide under. She slowly lifted each one to peek. The sixth time, she finally found a crawdad and quickly grabbed it behind its pinchers and dropped it into the duffle bag slung over her shoulder. She continued to work the rocks, and as she moved upstream, she found an area where the crawdads were under almost every three rocks. Some were pretty large. Finally satisfied with her haul, Mariah took her crawdads back to the creek bank where the herbs were still wilting in the sun. She needed to get some wood for a fire.

Putting on her shoes, she walked back to the spot where she had found the dead pine tree. Plenty of firewood limbs scattered the area. She gathered the sticks and some more of the pitch bark. She tried a different route back down to the river, hoping to find a path with less brush, which had been scratching up her legs.

HWOCK! Great Blue Heron, she thought. Looking in the direction of the sound, Mariah finally spotted not only the heron but a nest as well. She stared at it in awe. This set-ting felt like a part of her that had been missing. She loved natural places—it gave her a deep sense of home.

At the riverbank, Mariah began picking up rocks about the size of bowling balls to make a fire pit. Then she set three rocks in the center to make a tripod for the pan. The small branches plus the pitch bark caught fire right away, and after adding a few larger branches, Mariah had a small, fire going. She laid the pan, half-filled with water, on the three rocks in the center. Then, one at a time, she picked up a crawdad, pulled out the gut, and dropped it in.

Now Mariah sat back and basked in the pleasure of activities she had loved as a child. When the crawdads had boiled, she poured off the water and began peeling them. She had noticed a few flat boards tangled in some brush near the water. She pulled one of them out and washed it off in the stream to use as a cutting board. Then she chopped all the herbs, flowers, and berries she had collected into a colorful mash. She cut the crawdad meat into tiny pieces and mixed half the mash with it.

Just when she started wondering if Mark and Dick were ever coming back, Mariah heard them. As they drew near, she saw that Mark was holding a large smallmouth bass still flipping around in his hand. She trotted over to Mark, deftly threaded her finger through its gill to take it, and offered to clean it. Surprised, Mark let her take the fish. He turned to Dick with a grin, and said, "Where'd she learn to do that?" With wide eyes, Dick shrugged.

Mariah took the fish to her cutting board and began gutting it. Then she carefully cut behind the head and worked her knife down the backbone to the tail fin, flipped the fish over, and did the same thing on the other side. With the sides off the bones, she slid the knife under the skin, producing two boneless filets. Then she put some of her mash in the pan and set it over the fire. She laid the first filet over the mash and put all the chopped crawdads on top of the filet. She placed the other filet on top of the first and then smeared the rest of the mash on top of it all. After the bottom filet was cooked, she expertly flipped the whole thing over without disturbing the layers. The two men stood over her with their mouths agape.

Dick finally asked, "Where did this come from? I mean, how did you learn all these skills?"

Mariah smiled. "Did either of you bring plates?"

Dick scampered to the Jeep and brought out a cooler and a grocery bag. "I have sodas, paper plates, plastic utensils, and a bag of potato chips."

"My parents did a lot of camping and living off the land when I was young. We three did everything together. My mother was obsessed with Native American culture and traveled all over the U.S. studying different native groups. She believed she was a quarter Native American, but she never knew what tribe. My great-grandmother had a daughter by a man our family never knew. She refused to talk about him and didn't even acknowledge that he was Native American. But there was talk. My mother believed she looked Native American, too. She has dark straight hair and a ruddy tan complexion, although she was out in the sun so much, anyone would have that color skin.

"Anyway, we were always camping. Sometimes we even slept in a teepee. It was an exciting life, though. And now they are in South America somewhere studying a native culture. I haven't been able to contact them, and I wish I could. I miss them. A lot. This place reminded me how much."

With a chunk of fish still in his mouth, Mark asked, "What's this stuff in between the filets? Whatever it is, it tastes good."

"Crawdads. That's what we called them. Crayfish, crawfish, whatever. I cleaned and cooked them and then chopped them up with a bunch of herbs and berries I found in the woods."

"Well, I'll be," said Mark. "Did you get pinched?"

Mariah laughed. "No. You have to catch them behind the pinchers. They tend to scoot backward, so you have to be ready well behind them. And you have to be quick."

On the way home, Mariah curled up in the back seat with her eyes closed. Reliving her day and aching for her family. While her parents were gone, she had put them out of her mind, but now this fishing trip had lit up her memories—and her love for her family. The foraging experience had sparked a fire inside. A part of her true identity was resurfacing, and it felt like coming home.

She wanted to talk to her parents. Since she had failed to leave contact information back in Ohio, they probably didn't even know where she had gone.

The next morning, as soon as she woke, Mariah began to work on contacting her parents. She tried their old number first; in case they had kept it somehow. She got that familiar shriek with a message that the number had been disconnected. She wondered why they had to break your eardrums just to tell you the number's disconnected. Next, she thought about trying the university. She couldn't quite remember the number and had to call information to get it. That connected her with the main Ohio University operator. "Good Morning, Ohio University," said a cheerful voice.

"My parents are professors at OU. Do you have a listing for Claire McKenzie or Brent McKenzie?

"What department are they in?"

"Anthropology."

"I don't see a listing for them, but I could forward your call to the department office if you'd like."

"Yes, please"

"Anthropology, Jenna."

"Hi, my parents were on sabbatical from there, and I'm trying to contact them. Are they back yet?"

"Oh! Is this Mariah?"

"Yes. You've heard from them?"

"We got a letter from them just last week. The letter had been sent a couple of months ago but took a long time to get to us. It said they needed more time to stay with the natives. It took so long for them to imbed themselves that they can't leave just yet."

"That sounds like them. Would you please write down my address and phone number to give them as soon as they get back? Thanks."

By the time they get back, I'll have had the baby and be an unwed mother. That'll feel strange, but at least they will know where I am. I miss them so much!

Chapter Twenty-Four

Mariah couldn't wait for the next tutoring session with Ramona. Helping Ramona made Mariah feel needed, useful, and appreciated. Meanwhile, Dick Hansen Realty was full of activity. The closing for Betsy's house and her new home were to happen simultaneously in the same title office. Mariah arranged final walk-throughs and shepherded the paperwork.

Around three o'clock, Dick emerged from his office looking rushed. "I'm leaving early today. I have to go right now."

Mariah cocked her head to one side. "Hot date?"

"No! I'm taking a volunteer coaching position for a youth football team, and this is my first meeting. Junior high school kids. They're the best!

"Football?"

"Yes, football. I played all through junior high and high school. It's a great game and teaches a lot about leadership and working together as a team."

"You're doing a lot of volunteer work these days."

"It gives me pleasure. Gotta go."

Mariah had questioned Dick's volunteering, but now she understood the pleasure he was talking about. She left the office shortly afterward to do her own volunteer work. She was looking forward to it.

This time Ramona had some questions about finance, interest, and compounding, which had her cross-eyed with confusion, but Mariah was the perfect person to help make it all clear. The coaching took a lot longer than the last time but was worth it for both of them. Mariah left with more confidence in herself, and Ramona finally felt she could pass a math exam.

The weekend was approaching, and Alex was coming over to Mariah's to plan the baby shower. When Saturday came, Alex brought over decorations and some games to play. She also helped Mariah clean out the spare room to turn it into a baby's room. Once the room was tidied, it was clear to them it needed paint. They ran out to the hardware store. Mariah couldn't decide on a color, since she didn't know what gender the baby would be. They settled for blue, yellow, and orange.

On the way back, Alex suggested they stop at the Goodwill. There they found an inexpensive little dresser and crib. Fortunately, they'd bought enough paint to redo the furniture.

The two friends painted all afternoon and into the evening. They had a lot of laughs deciding which color to paint which surface. Mariah commented that the room looked so wonderful, it made the rest of the house seem drab.

"Well, now that you know the magic of paint, you can transform the rest of the house yourself," said Alex with a grin.

"I'm starved," said Mariah. "And I don't have anything to feed you."

"You don't have to feed me. Why don't we pick up a pizza or call it in for delivery?"

Mariah laughed. "Let's call it in. That way we don't have to do anything more. I'm not just hungry—I'm exhausted."

Alex had sent invitations to everyone on Dick's list. The shower was scheduled for the following Saturday. She also invited Ramona and told her not to think about a gift—just her presence would be special for Mariah. The list was much longer than Alex had imagined, so she set the time for the shower as a range between one and four o'clock.

In the middle of the week, Mariah met Betsy and the Nelsons for the closing. It went smoothly, and Mariah was about to receive the biggest commission of her career—seller/buyer commission on Betsy's old house and buyer commission on Betsy's new home. After the closing, the soon-to-be-rich Mariah took Betsy out for lunch. The two exchanged congratulatory high-fives as they sat down for some salad niçoise at a nearby hotel.

"Do you have any more ideas on how our thoughts bring about the physical world?" asked Mariah.

"I never said our thoughts bring about the physical world. All I said last time we talked was that our sensory perception limits what we can experience, and our brains compose a story to make sense of what we think, see, and feel. Our thoughts bring about our story. And our story uses the jumble of 'stuff' we think is our physical world as the staging, you might say, for the story. It's complicated for us to wrap our heads around because of how little we perceive."

"Oh," said Mariah, "I guess I'm trying to connect it with manifesting."

"Okay. What if everything we think we want in the physical world was already here," suggested Betsy. "Manifesting would then be more a matter of recognition."

"So, you're saying that our thoughts don't create our reality then?"

"Give me an example of something you want to create."

"What about a husband?"

"You don't think you can create a husband from scratch, do you? A husband has to start as a baby and grow up over years and years, right?"

"Yes."

"Think of the components to your desired manifestation as already being here. Have you ever played with a kaleidoscope?"

"Many times. I love those things!"

"Well, you know all the little glass chips in the kaleidoscope are already there in the scope, right? And every time you turn it, you get a different picture, even though it's always the same chips in the kaleidoscope."

"I have to admit, Betsy, that gives me a new perspective. But what about when bad things happen? I've just spent months dealing with some ugly pictures in my reality."

"I believe there's a force we all carry with us that acts like static electricity. It can attract and repel things and people around us. In the kaleidoscope analogy, you might say the static causes the chips to clump up, making the same stuff go round and round, over and over. If the static is from negative beliefs, the clumped chips show up all the time and mask the ones we might want to see. If the beliefs are positive around what we want, then those things are more likely to come to the front."

"I don't want to deal with those negative ones anymore. I might want to throw the whole kaleidoscope away and start over. Why can't I turn it to see a different picture?"

"You can. It's the gift of time. We get a new picture every new increment of time. Let's say, every day. Each full turn of the earth gives us a new picture unless our thoughts and beliefs persist in keeping those clumps together. You would need to demagnetize the old beliefs."

"Well, I don't think I can just ignore all the bad stuff that has happened to me."

"Maybe kaleidoscope is too simple an analogy. Try this one out. Imagine everyone made a picture of how they wanted their life to look. Then each picture was cut into a jigsaw puzzle, dumped out, and mixed up with all the pictures from everyone else. The picture you want is already there, but it's in lots of little pieces jumbled with other people's pieces. If you pick up a piece that doesn't match your picture, you know it must be for someone else. You put it back down, but you don't get angry or depressed about it. Everything you need for your picture is already there, you just have to pick up the right pieces. And holding the picture in your mind makes it much easier to recognize the right ones. When you come across a piece that doesn't match your picture, you just drop it and let it go. No need to have an emotional reaction to it."

"It must be a four-dimensional jigsaw puzzle, too."

"Right," said Betsy, as they left the restaurant.

Knowing the commission check wouldn't be ready until the next day, Mariah decided to go to a park and maybe take a walk and relax. Centennial Park was nearby, and the terrain was more or less flat, so walking in her enlarged condition was a lot easier. She made a one-mile loop and then sat on a bench to relax. Several families were playing in the grassy area. Mariah watched them intently. She focused on their interactions and the fun they were having. Mothers tended babies on blankets while fathers played ball with their sons. A little girl climbed on one of the structures until she fell, prompting her father to run over, pick her up, and bring the child to her mother. Father and Mother cuddled and kissed her until she stopped crying.

Families, thought Mariah. This is the picture of what I want.

Her attention was taken up with two families near her for over an hour, watching them laugh and play. She had begun noticing the men in families. The longing for a husband built inside her until her heart ached. She felt grief for the part of her dream that was missing. It was the grieving of expectation being ripped away. Where was the man who would fit into *her* dream? It still seemed impossible, as she had yet to spot a likely person. It seemed to her that if a man was with a woman, he was married or committed. But if he was not married or committed, then he wasn't the kind of family man she wanted.

When she got home, Sombra kitty was begging for food and then wanted to cuddle, but Mariah was in no mood for a kitty. She wanted a man. Someone to be her partner and help her through this unfamiliar time of having a baby and learning to do motherhood. Where was *that* puzzle piece?

When Alex arrived on Saturday to set up for the party, the two chatted as they hung baby decorations.

"Betsy made an interesting comment when I saw her this week," said Mariah.

"What was that?" asked Alex, who was on a step stool at the other end of the pink and blue streamers they were putting up.

"She said everything we want is already here. She likened it to a kaleidoscope where all the chips are already in the thing, but as you turn it you see different pictures. And then she said it was more like every person's picture of what they want all cut up into jigsaw puzzles and dumped out in a mixed-up pile. Aw, heck. I can't remember it well enough to make sense."

Alex pondered for a few minutes. "I think she is trying to say it's all a matter of perception."

"Okay, I get it. But how can a person change their perception?"

"Back to the forgiveness, Mariah."

"You mean not forgiving is keeping me from having a new perception?"

"Bingo." Alex climbed down from the step stool. "It's not just a matter of seeing what we want. You also have to knock down some of those beliefs that block the perception of what's already there. Forgiving is just releasing or dissolving those blocks."

At two-thirty, a few guests started to trickle in. Clara and then Mark showed up with wrapped gifts. Alex had brought cookies and a veggie plate with dip. There were two punches; one was blue and the other was pink. Mariah showed Mark and Clara the baby's room and laid the gifts there. They were soft and small, most likely onesies.

Around three, more people came all at once. Sara and Dar surprised Mariah, who didn't know who had been invited. Several other guests showed up from Jackson & Verrone.

Hannah brought her little Brendon, who was a tank by then. Mariah wondered if her baby would be that large at eleven months. If so, could she even lift him? The guests piled their gifts in the baby's room and then started playing blindfolded-pin-the-diaper-on-the-baby and some guessing games.

When it was time to start opening presents, Alex went to her car and brought in a large, wrapped gift. Mariah opened it right away to find a changing table. Other gifts were toys, tiny clothing, little blankets, and the like. Mariah was over-whelmed by her friends' generosity. The baby's room was filled with colorful and useful items. Mariah thanked and hugged all the guests. She was in tears of gratitude.

As the party was winding down, Betsy arrived with her new girlfriend. They brought a gift for the baby and an almond cream cheese pastry. "This is something I like to make for brunches, and I made it in my new kitchen," Betsy explained. Party guests descended on the pastry—not out of hunger, but for its delicious aroma. Everyone was raving about it. Betsy said she couldn't wait for Mariah to open their gift, so they went into the baby's room, while the remaining guests emptied the pastry plate. Inside colorful wrapping was a kaleidoscope that operated with a motor, beaming images onto the ceiling. "I love it!" Mariah said. "Until the baby is born, the kaleidoscope will live in *my* bed-room. Then, after the baby comes, *maybe* I'll give it back."

After the guests left, Alex helped Mariah clean up and put things away. "I can't thank you enough, Alex. You did so much to make this wonderful. I wish there was something I could do for you."

"Don't misunderstand giving, Mariah. Giving to others gives more to the giver than the receiver. And as we're all connected in some way, giving to anyone positively affects everyone."

"But why does the giver get more than the receiver?"

"Because the giver gives with a full heart without any expectation, while the receiver can only receive as much as he or she is open to. The giver gets to walk away from the interaction happy and full of light and love."

When Alex left, Mariah was eager to set up the kaleidoscope in her bedroom. She positioned it so the full mandala would fit her ceiling above the bed. She wondered what Sombra would think of it. At bedtime, she turned it on and lay on her back to watch it change. In the beginning, she found herself judging each design. This one is nice ... meh, that one's boring ... ooh, that one is the best ever, and so forth. Realizing it was all the same chips just rearranging themselves, she let go of the desire to judge them and allowed the show to move along. They were all beautiful and Mariah felt herself filled with gratitude over everything.

In the morning, Mariah was still thinking about the lessons of the previous day, especially the lesson from the kaleidoscope—letting go of judgment and allowing each day to unfold with gratitude. And she had a new awareness of the role giving played. Mariah thought about Ramona, whose needs were so much greater than her own. She decided to buy Ramona a gift. She also wanted to buy gifts for Betsy and the Nelsons.

Mariah was eager to give Ramona the cute baby things she had gotten for her but didn't know where Ramona lived. That would have to wait until Monday. And then, on Monday she couldn't get away from work on time. Arriving at the high school around five o'clock, Mariah found Ramona as she was just leaving. As Mariah gave her the gifts, Ramona looked troubled. "Alex invited me to your shower and said I didn't need to bring a gift, but I was ashamed to come. And I was afraid I would be in the way since I wouldn't know anyone except you and Alex."

"You would have been welcome and not in the way at all, but I understand, Ramona. And I'm learning that giving is the most joyful part. Please accept these gifts because it would make me so happy."

"Thank you," said Ramona. "I desperately need so many things for the baby. And I'm also worried about where we will live. I can't stay with my friend when the baby comes, and to move anywhere else I can afford might be impossible. I don't even have a job."

"I'll keep you in my thoughts, Ramona. Your situation is pretty complicated. What kind of things do you like to do? Maybe it would stimulate some ideas we could work on for a job."

"I like to garden. I've even been doing some weeding at my friend's house to help pay them back for letting me stay there."

"I'll give that some thought, Ramona." Mariah went home basking in the joy of giving.

Chapter Twenty-Five

Arthur waited patiently for Mariah to leave. He didn't want to see her. He had avoided talking to or even looking at her since discovering the truth about her condition. He couldn't stand to see her enormous belly advertising the imminent birth of the child he had caused. He didn't even see himself as the cause of it. Some other part of him that he rejected caused it. He would kill that part if he could.

He saw her slip out the front door and head to the office. Now he could work freely in the yard. He loved tending that landscape. He loved the soil in his hands. Each plant had an individual personality and he spoke to all of them as friends. The yard had no lawn to speak of. Instead, flower beds surrounded a large stone patio. He had added most of the flowers himself, one at a time.

Today, he brought out some white vinegar and poured it along all the cracks in the patio to kill the weeds. Then he began pulling any weeds he found in the beds and clipped all the fading flowers. He paid special attention to his favorite rose, a Double Delight, which exuded intense perfume.

As he worked, he felt his peacefulness slip away. He loved his landscape but knew he had to leave this place. It was difficult to avoid Mariah, and he did not want to see the baby. He would go before it came.

He had prayed for forgiveness, and he knew he had to get rid of the angry part of himself, but he didn't know how. He asked God to take it away, but he felt it was still there. He would ask again. And again.

Next, he walked to the other three rentals Mariah had hired him to maintain. The houses were not far from each other, no more than three blocks between each. He carried his hula-hoe, a rake, and a soil knife. These were simpler, plain landscapes with lawns and perennial shrubs. One of the houses had a lawn mower stored there, and he dragged it and his tools from house to house, starting with the one farthest out and working his way back.

He worked quickly, first mowing and weeding the lawn, then weeding the beds. Being without an edging tool, he used his soil knife to separate the lawn from the beds where the grass had encroached. He raked the weeds and stray leaves into a pile and put them in the renter's garbage can.

When he reached the last house, where he stored the lawn mower, he noticed a landscape maintenance rig parked in the adjacent driveway. He continued mowing and weeding, looking up from time to time at the worker next door, who was looking back at him.

The two finished about the same time and the worker walked over to introduce himself to Arthur.

"Hi, I'm Henry," said the burly man with buzzcut hair.

"Arthur," shaking hands.

"I've seen you before. You do good work—fast and efficient."

"These are simple to do, so I work fast. But there is one I take my time with," Arthur said, smiling.

"You should work with me. I have a rig and all the tools you need. We could combine our jobs and get more. We could make a lot of money."

"I don't know if I can do that. I need to get a job that pays enough for me to find an apartment. These jobs don't pay squat."

"Why don't you just try it out for a week? We could see how we work together and then we could talk about the money." Henry spat a wad of brown liquid into the grass.

"I guess that wouldn't be too bad. With your equipment, we could do these jobs in no time at all."

"That's what I thought. Why don't I pick you up at your place on Monday morning at eight?"

"No, not my place. You could pick me up here at this house and we'll go from there."

"Okay, whatever. See you then."

Henry met Arthur the next Monday and they made quick work of the landscapes. Henry had an edger and mower. He used herbicide on the weeds. He carried a large can for the grass clippings and leaves. It only took a few hours to finish up.

Afterward, they ate lunch together in Henry's truck. With a large bite of sandwich in his mouth, Henry said, "See how fast it goes with two people?"

"Of course," said Arthur, "but most of these jobs are yours. How would we split the money?"

"I've been thinking about that. I have most of the jobs and I have the truck and trailer and all the equipment. But you work just as hard as I do, so you need to be paid for your time. Maybe I could give you twenty-five percent. And what about getting more jobs? We get things done so fast, we could get twice as many accounts. Would you work on lining some up?"

"No way. I can't talk to people that way."

"Then I'll get more jobs. But I need your commitment. If we have twice as many jobs, then I wouldn't be able to keep up without you."

"There's something I have to tell you," said Arthur. "I don't get paid much money for these three jobs. I get a place to live and a small amount of money for food is all. The thing is, I can't stay in that place any longer, so I'm going to have to find a new apartment, and I won't have these jobs. I'll have to make a lot of money to pay for rent on a new place."

"Geez, I hardly know you, and now it all sounds complicated."

"Right. I just don't see how this could work out."

"You'll get a job, no problem with the way you hustle. No doubt about that. I wish I could pay you enough to make this work, but you know, the gigs I have now just pay my rent, so I was counting on getting enough more jobs to add to my income and pay you. How long could you hang on? Long enough for me to get some more work?"

"Not long at all. Maybe just a few days, but I still don't have any job prospects."

Henry stared into the distance. "I live alone. I have a spare bedroom I use when my kids visit, but they live so far away that hardly ever happens. You could stay at my place, if that would work, to give us more time to build the business."

"Let me think about it. In the meantime, at least I'll finish out the week with you."

Because she was approaching her due date, Mariah wasn't working on getting any new listings. She was so huge she couldn't even take a deep breath with the baby crowding up under her ribs. She had a hard time sleeping and felt tired all the time. The others at the office were plenty busy, though. Clara had orchestrated a cascade of closings. Marla had several closings of her own. And Mark was wheeling and dealing over several rental properties with his investor friends.

At the same time, Dick was planning his annual office picnic in Edwin Warner Park. He asked Mariah to make a flyer. She wondered, why make a flyer for the eight or so agents in the office? Couldn't they just tell everyone? Nevertheless, she made the flyers and put them in envelopes to mail to the agents.

"Where is Edwin Warner Park?" Mariah asked Dick. "Is it close to Percy Warner Park? Are the two Warners related?"

"Edwin and Percy were brothers. Edwin Warner Park is just a little farther out than your favorite park and it has rental picnic structures. We don't need a large one, but it's nice and there are walking paths around it. I think you'll like it."

Mariah hoped she would be able to attend. The baby could come any day, although she estimated she could have as much as two weeks. She'd had a meeting with Wymeena, the midwife—a large woman with kind eyes and a gentle touch. When they met and Wymeena reached out to shake her hand, it felt to Mariah that the two of them had melted into each other as one. Wymeena swayed in her bold-flowered muumuu as she checked Mariah out. She felt the orientation of the baby and the approximate size. Her deft X-ray fingers were able to describe everything about the baby. Mariah was to call Wymeena the minute she felt the labor spasms start. Wymeena described how labor would feel and warned Mariah that she could experience back labor, which might feel like gas pains.

Once Mariah's labor started, they would be in constant contact, and Wymeena would make sure the room in her house was scheduled for the right moment. Mariah could come there any time after labor started and relax in the living room until her contractions intensified.

Arthur was beginning to trust Henry. A down-to-earth guy with a great sense of humor, he smiled all the time. Arthur realized he didn't mind when Henry corrected him. If he did something Henry didn't like, he'd say, "Here, let me show you how I do it. And this is why it's better." It was so different from the people he'd worked for in the past, especially the women. They would yell at him and tell him he was dumb. Arthur thought Henry would be a fine room-mate, as long as he didn't smoke too much. He noticed that Henry chewed tobacco when he was on the job, so as not to offend any of his clients.

On Friday, Henry met Arthur with a big smile. He was always smiling, but this one was more like beaming. "I got us three more clients! Please tell me you will stay and join me in the business."

Arthur nodded. He didn't know how he would tell Mariah he was leaving, but he had to. It wasn't so much leaving the jobs that he dreaded. It was facing the woman he didn't want to see to explain it to her. He fantasized about just leaving a note. It was also hard to say goodbye to his yard. He couldn't leave it a note.

The next morning Arthur walked around the yard while Mariah was still sleeping. He touched each of his plants, admiring the ones in flower and thanking them for being so beautiful. He knew they wouldn't look beautiful much longer, with no one there to put energy into weeding and fertilizing.

It was a hot August weekend. To avoid Mariah, as well as stay cool, Arthur went to a park to lie under a shade tree the rest of the afternoon. He returned home at dusk. There wasn't much to pack. He folded his clothing into a box and put non-perishable food and a few plates and utensils in another box. When Henry came on Sunday, they would be ready.

That night Arthur prayed more fervently than he ever had. He asked God to forgive him for what he had done. He told God that he wanted to be free from the pain and hatred that lived inside him. He went on like this until he fell asleep.

On Saturday, Mariah went to the park looking for Alex. She was easy to find and the two of them sat on a bench together.

"To tell you the truth, I'm scared," Mariah confided. "I don't know what life is going to be like. I never saw myself as being a single mother, raising a child on my own."

"What do you need, Mariah?"

"It just isn't fair—to be forced into this position of being alone, having a baby without a partner. A week or so ago, I watched some families as they played with their children. They supported each other when they needed to discipline a child or care for one when she was crying. It all seemed so natural and perfect."

"How's the forgiveness going?"

"You would bring that up. How can I forgive the rapist when he's the one causing me to be an unwed mother?"

"We've been through this before, haven't we? Forgiveness is not about the other person. It's about how *you* react to things that happen to you. It's about rules you make for how you interact with men and your expectations of them. When you forgive, you release those rules that block you from having the relationships you want. The rapist is not the only one blocking you from that."

"Well, you're right. My last boyfriend wanted everything to lead to sex. If we went to a party, he wanted me to wear a sexy dress, get drunk, and then go home and have sex. If I was upset, he would comfort me only until he could get his hands under my clothes."

"Similarly, your ex-boyfriend is not blocking you."

Mariah fell silent.

Finally, Alex said, "What would happen if you didn't have this attitude about men?"

Mariah took a deep belly breath.

"That's right, Mariah. I can see you relax with that thought. What's blocking you is the meaning you've made of those events."

"I can't think of another way to see it."

"Can you think of it having no meaning?"

"Maybe, but right now I still feel angry and scared."

"Give your anger and your fear to that part of you that's connected to The Universe. Tell it you don't have any good use for this condemnation and ask that a higher part of yourself help let it go. And then think about the relationship you *want* to have. If you do it with sincerity, it will work."

Mariah went home and prayed. This time she let the pain of being alone build up in her until she could barely stand it. Then she willed that pain to build even more until, like an overblown balloon, it popped. At that moment, she was ready to surrender anything that prevented her from having that loving family relationship she yearned for. In her mind, she spoke directly to what she still referred to as The Universe. *I'm ready. Please help me release these blocks to your love. Wash away everything that prevents me from having a loving relationship with a man. Let it be someone who will see me for who I am. Someone who wants a family. Someone who appreciates what I have to offer and supports me.*

Chapter Twenty-Six

Sunday morning Arthur said a final goodbye to his landscape plants, tenderly touching each, willing them to thrive.

Then he began cleaning his cottage. He took out the throw carpets and beat them with a large branch until they no longer yielded dust. They belonged to Arthur, but he decided to leave them with the place. He cleaned the refrigerator, throwing out any perishable food he didn't expect to eat, and carefully scrubbed it inside and out. He used his leftover white vinegar to dissolve the calcium buildup in the shower and make everything look as new as possible. The floor came last. He swept and mopped the linoleum floor with an old towel until the ridiculous brown and gold design clearly showed. Now he was ready to load Henry's truck and leave. But of course, he still needed to wait until Mariah got up to tell her he was leaving.

Mariah slept in as long as she could. Sunday morning meant there was nothing she needed to do unless she had an open house. With no new listings, she could get up when she wanted. She didn't sleep well these days. It was hard to breathe lying on her back, so side-sleeping was the only option. But that, too, made her back ache after a while and she had to switch sides often. It felt like forever since she'd had a deep sleep. It was August, however, so soon the rising sun turned her bedroom into an oven, and she got up.

Shuffling into the kitchen, she noticed Arthur industriously beating his rugs with a stick. She prepared her bowl of oatmeal with raisins, walnuts, and cinnamon, and sat down to eat. The baby made a slow, deliberate move to the side and stretched out a foot, which produced a bump she could feel with her hand. She caressed it, imagining the fat little foot with cornrow toes—her favorite baby part.

Mariah felt more relaxed than she could ever remember. The world looked more beautiful, and the air felt clean. She noticed the stunning flowers in the yard and decided to go out and pick some of the roses. Searching for a vase, she finally settled on an empty wine bottle for a single bloom. As she headed toward the Double Delight rose, Arthur grabbed his clippers and intercepted her.

"Here, let me show you how to cut the roses," he said. "You choose one."

Mariah did.

"Now look down for a leaf node that points in an outward direction. You want to cut here, so the next growth from that stem doesn't interfere with the other branches of the plant. And then cut at an angle like this," as he placed the clippers slightly above the leaf, pointing downward, and clipped the rose. He rubbed off all the thorns before handing it to Mariah.

"Thank you, Arthur. I always wondered about the proper way to clip roses."

Looking down and fidgeting, Arthur twisted his body right and left. "I need to tell you that I'm leaving today. Moving out."

"Oh, Arthur, I'm sorry to hear that," said Mariah. "You've done such a wonderful job with the landscapes. I'm not sure how we'll manage without you."

At that moment, Arthur looked up, catching eye contact with the one person he had so carefully avoided. With the rose held between them, he saw a light forming so bright it overpowered the sun. The light's intensity bore no heat as it enveloped both of them and expanded outward as if to surround the entire world.

Mariah saw ghostly hands caress Arthur's face and a voice in her head whispered, *Precious.* Waves of love channeled through her and rippled out to infinity. She didn't want this feeling to ever end, but Arthur turned and went back into his apartment. Walking into her house, Mariah set the rose down on the kitchen table. Her diaphragm quivered, as she choked back tears. Then she let the tears come anyway, as she asked herself, *what was that?*

Soon Henry pulled into the back alley and loaded Arthur's belongings. The two of them drove off, leaving an empty but clean cottage behind Mariah's house.

Mariah immediately picked up the phone to dial Alex. She got no answer, so she headed to the park to catch Alex at the end of her run. Mariah had to wait a half hour before she finally saw her, sweaty strands of hair stuck together in wet ringlets escaping from her cap.

"If you want to talk, can you walk with me for a bit?" Alex asked. "I need a cool down right away."

"Sure," said Mariah. She noticed she felt lighter, but with a lower center of gravity, as if the baby was shifting downward. It made walking easier, and she seemed to have more energy.

As they walked, Mariah began to describe her experience with Arthur—the ghostly hands, the whisper, the waves of energy that felt like love. "What do you think it means?"

"Hard to say what it means. I feel in awe."

"But do you think it has anything to do with forgiveness?"

"Undoubtedly. Forgiveness releases the blocks to the awareness of Love's presence."

"So, I guess my prayers last night for forgiveness were answered this morning. I'm afraid though. It makes me think Arthur must be the rapist. What do you think?"

"Not necessarily. You experienced Oneness. That includes everyone. The fact that it was Arthur in front of you only means he was ready for that experience, too."

"Do you think he felt it as well, then?"

"It's possible—it's hard to know. You can never know what's going on inside another person."

"Wow. I still can't get over it. This is an experience I'll never forget. Has it ever happened to you?"

"A few times, though not exactly the same. I don't know why it's so difficult to have it all the time. When it happens to me, it always follows the release of something stuck within. Because I remember those experiences so vividly, your description triggered a yearning for it to happen again for me."

"So, I guess this means I may have forgiven what men have done to me."

"That may well be."

By now the two had arrived back at the park entrance where they found their favorite bench unoccupied. Alex stretched while Mariah sat at the other end.

Alex asked, "What do you feel when you think about your experiences with men now?"

"I still remember, only not the same way. I remember being attacked, but not the part I didn't actually experience. Like, the parts I made up about the rapist just don't exist anymore. And I remember the way my boyfriend Jack acted, but I just don't have any more feelings about it. It just is. Or was. Thanks for letting me talk this out. I feel great! And I think I might be ready to find my mate."

"Believe me, Mariah, it has been my pleasure. And it helped me as much as it did you. Good luck with the mate discovery."

Mariah went home feeling happy and calm, despite the rapid turn of events. She picked up Sombra and cuddled him for a while.

The next day at the office, Mariah met with Dick right away to tell him about Arthur moving out. "Arthur didn't say whether he would still maintain the rentals, and I'm not sure how to reach him since he left so suddenly."

Dick offered to drive by the rentals the following Monday to see if Arthur was still caring for them.

"Oh, I just thought of something I'd like to run by you, Dick."

"Go ahead—shoot."

"Well, since Arthur's little cottage is now vacant, and we need someone to keep up the landscape, what if I invite Ramona to come live there and take care of the yard? She's a girl I've been helping with tutoring to finish high school while she's pregnant. She's been sleeping on her friend's couch, and that can't continue much longer. She told me she likes to garden. What do you think?"

"We need to get someone in there. Can you vouch for her? And if she doesn't work out, will you be willing to kick her out? I like the idea that you are helping her, but we don't want to be stuck with her if she doesn't take care of the yard after all."

"I feel pretty confident that she will be fine. And I want her to have a place to be with her baby when it comes."

"Okay, then. It's your job to handle these rentals as you see fit."

Most of the realtors were busiest on the weekends, so Dick had scheduled the picnic for a Wednesday. Mariah organized the list of things others would bring so that anyone who called or came by later would know what items were still needed. The invited agents dropped by to talk to Mariah and Dick about it. They offered to bring certain dishes, like salads, fruit, and desserts. Dick had already committed to bringing plates and utensils, buns, and meat for the barbecue.

Mark invited Mariah to visit the picnic site ahead of time to help plan what activities would be fun and practical for the space. Mariah agreed quickly because she was eager to see it for the first time. Upon arriving, they found the spot, noting that it had a long, covered picnic table and barbecue right next to a grassy area where they could do any sort of game they wanted. Mark didn't want to have any sack races but offered to bring a soccer ball and a football. The guests had few children to keep happy, so adult games were best.

Before they left the park, Mark took a turn to a different area.

"Watch this," he said. He clicked off the engine and shifted into neutral. The car started rolling uphill!

"Wait, what?" Mariah shrieked.

"It's an illusion. It only looks like we're going uphill, but it's freaky, right?"

"An illusion—reminding us that what we think we experience is not necessarily truth. How deep."

Mark gave her a puzzled look but said nothing.

On the day of the picnic, no one was at the office, as they were all getting ready, making their potato or fruit salad and other goodies. Dick picked up the burgers, hot dogs, and buns. He also brought a large watermelon, packed with ice in a cooler.

Mariah was concerned about going into labor while at the picnic; however, she felt it was important to be there with the folks at the office since this was a special annual event. Every time she had a twinge of any kind, she would stop and wait to see what was going to happen next. She laughed that she had better not eat the baked beans or she would be rushing off to the midwife for nothing.

The crowd at the picnic was larger than Mariah had expected. The agents at the office brought their families, and Dick had also invited a few other people—some of whom had previously been under Dick's realtor umbrella. The picnic was a good opportunity for Mariah to get to know some of the agents she didn't see much, like Marla, for instance, who never came to the office except to turn in some paperwork. The guests all began to clump into smaller groups. Some wanted to kick around the soccer ball, some just wanted to sit and gossip. Pretty soon Mariah sat alone on the picnic bench.

The men were playing "skins versus shirts" football. Dick played on the shirtless team and Mariah noticed how fit he looked as he deftly wove past shirted defenders, respectful of the others' level of skill, which kept the game fun for everyone.

Later, Dick invited Mariah to walk around on some of the trails. She hesitated. In case her labor started, she didn't want to go too far, but she did need to walk off some of the food.

Dick assured her they would go no farther than they could get back quickly to her car. Mariah was curious about Edwin Warner Park, so they began an easy walk into the woods.

As they walked, Mariah commented that Dick hadn't brought anyone with him. "What happened to that woman, I think her name was Patsy?"

"Oh, I never saw her again. She's not my type. She was just someone a friend of mine tried to set me up with."

"Really? What *is* your type?"

"Well, here goes. She'll be smart. Not conceited about it, or overly analytical, but able to pick up concepts—someone who can have an intelligent conversation with me. And she would have a sweet, loving kind of personality. Not necessarily big on showy looks. More natural. Someone who loves nature. And most importantly, someone who wants a family. That's what I want most of all."

Dick looked at Mariah and noticed her furrowed brow and squinting eyes as she cocked her head to the side, staring at him.

"I know what you're thinking, Mariah; and I promise you, I understand how you feel about intra-office relationships and I respect your beliefs on that."

As they began walking again, Mariah felt a sort of dizziness she couldn't explain. She felt almost faint. Dick had just described *her* as the woman he wanted to be with. And as she looked at it in that light, he fit her image of the man she wanted, too. *Have I just blocked a great relationship from happening? Where did I get that idea about intra-office relationships being bad, anyway?* Then she remembered her first boss at the insurance company, who, while married, had an affair with his secretary. They both ended up losing their jobs and he had a divorce. *Does that have to influence how I live my life? Will it control my happiness?* She quickly asked her higher self to help her lose this belief, if it was in her best interest to do so. She began to breathe more slowly. The blood returned to her head. As they continued walking, Mariah shyly put her hand into Dick's. He gave her hand a gentle squeeze and stroked the back of her fingers with his thumb. He closed his eyes for a moment and then faced Mariah with a loving smile and looked into her eyes.

"You're fired," said Dick.

* * *

Epilogue

Mariah and Dick sat holding hands on Wymeena's couch, staring ahead. Dick tried to make light conversation to keep the two of them relaxed, but Mariah just continued sitting stiffly, waiting for the next contraction. When her breathing became more forceful, Dick dutifully checked his watch and calculated the time since her last contraction. Four minutes. Light drifty piano music played hypnotically, and Wymeena lit a stick of incense, which was also supposed to contribute to a relaxed atmosphere. Still, Mariah was anything but relaxed.

Dick asked, "What's that music you're playing, Wymeena?"

"This is a new album from an artist I've never heard of named Jim Chappell. I like to buy new music, so I have lots of choices and I have a friend who scouts for unknown stuff like this. Dick, would you like to go out and get yourself something to eat? I'll stay and keep Mariah company while you're gone. It will be quite a while before anything new happens."

"I guess that would be a good idea," said Dick. "Mariah, would you like anything?"

Wymeena held her hand up, palm facing Dick in a stop gesture. "Mariah's body is busy pushing out a baby, so she won't be eating until after the birth."

Dick leaned toward Mariah and kissed her forehead. "I'll be back in a jiffy. Wymeena, the last contraction was at one-seventeen."

After Dick left, Wymeena took a long look at Mariah. "Dear, you look as stiff as a board. Speaking of board, how about a game? Something to get your mind off whatever is making you so tense?"

"I'm having trouble letting go. I'm afraid of the pain. I'm afraid to see what the baby looks like. I guess I just dread the unknown of it all." Just then, Mariah arched her back slightly and heaved a big sigh.

Wymeena put her hand on Mariah's belly and pushed in slightly. "We're getting closer. I'll put you in the room for delivery as soon as Dick comes back. What did you imagine giving birth would be like?"

"Well, I sure didn't imagine the way the whole thing happened. I thought I would get married and then have children, maybe three. I wanted a natural childbirth and breastfeeding, you know? This one is all backward. I don't know who the father is and wouldn't want to. I've forgiven the rapist for my own sake—not his. And I know this is going to be my baby. I'm grateful for Dick. He's been so sweet and loving. And he's already talking about marriage, so maybe my whole dream is coming true, just not how I had planned it. I'm glad he's keen to help me through the delivery and after. I'm so lucky to have him."

"He's a real prize, Mariah. I've known him for a long time. He sold me this house."

Just then the door opened, and Dick walked in holding a sandwich in his mouth. He sat next to Mariah on the couch and put his arm around her shoulders.

Wymeena said, "Mariah was just telling me how worried she is about the pain of birthing. The best thing you can do, Mariah, is relax. Tension causes more pain. Dick, would you be able to work on releasing the places she's holding the most tension? I know you're pretty good at massage."

Dick had Mariah scoot around and began to work on relaxing her shoulders and back. Mariah sighed deeply. "You're right, Wymeena. "He's more than pretty good."

Wymeena busied herself with setting up the bed in the birthing room. She had stacked loads of pillows at the head of the bed so Mariah could sit up at a forty-five-degree angle. Multiple pillows allowed her to fill in any gaps, helping Mariah be supported completely in whatever position was most comfortable. The room was air-conditioned to be slightly cold, the way hospitals are, and a stack of light blankets lay on a table next to the bed. Wymeena put absorbent pads with plastic backing on the bed and then a sheet on top of that. There were stools on both sides of the bed. One would be for Wymeena and the other for Dick. Wymeena was grateful knowing that Dick could be directed to assist her in any way she needed.

After the latest contraction, Dick said, "I went to your house to grab lunch since it was closer. Your phone rang, so I answered it."

"Who was it?"

"Your parents. They're back! I told them I was your fiancé. I hope you don't mind. And I informed them you were having a baby right now. They were excited, as you can imagine. They seemed so nice and accepting of me—us. I wrote their number down for you to call as soon as we get home. They want to come visit right away. Leaving tomorrow. I'll prepare a spare room for them before they get here tomorrow night.

And we can bring the baby home to my house as well. Mark is going to move the baby's things to my house so we can all be together. Do you feel okay about that?"

Tears welled up in Mariah's lids and her chest began to heave. In a strained voice, she said, "I miss them so much. I'm glad we can all be together. Thank you."

Another contraction had Dick calling Wymeena to ask if they should be going into the birthing room now.

"Come on in, do you need my help?"

Mariah staggered in, supported by Dick holding her left elbow and right shoulder. Dick helped her onto the bed, and Wymeena moved her feet and legs. Then she started shoving smaller pillows into any crevice. "Is that comfortable?"

"I'm still afraid of the pain. That last contraction was stronger. I don't think I can take it if it keeps getting worse."

Dick asked, "Do you remember telling me how Alex helped you with pain when you first met her?"

"It was about being in the present moment. How could I forget? But it was also a throbbing headache, do you think it could work on this?"

"Why not? How do you feel right now, in this moment?"

"Silly! It's between contractions."

"Right. Focus on that feeling and let yourself relax into it. Take some deep breaths. I'll be right here with you the whole time," said Dick.

Wymeena silently moved her lips in a "thank you."

"See," said Dick, "fear is about the future. When you are in the now, you can relax and savor the good feeling. Then when a contraction comes, you can focus on the movement of the baby coming out—into the world."

A contraction caused Mariah to whimper and twist. Dick instinctively put his hand on her back and found a cramped muscle. He massaged it gently until it relaxed.

"What would I do without you? That helped a lot," said Mariah.

"I don't want to contemplate the answer to that," said Dick. "I don't plan for you to ever be without me."

The next contraction was strong. Wymeena reminded Mariah to breathe the way she had taught her. Quick short breaths like panting helped her get through it. Wymeena said, "I see the head almost crowning. Before the next contraction, Dick, would you help me turn Mariah on her side? Then switch sides and let Mariah lay her upper leg on your shoulder. That will give me good access to the birth, and you will get a good view, too. Mariah, this next contraction do not try to push. I'm going to massage the perineum. We want it to stretch, not tear."

"What if it tears?"

"Well, I've midwifed hundreds of births without a tear. But don't worry. If it does, I know how to stitch it back up. Just don't push yet and we'll be alright."

At the next contraction, Wymeena continued massaging, and Mariah did the best she could to hold off pushing. The subsequent contraction advanced the baby's head, and Wymeena said, "*Push*! One more contraction, *push*!"

Wymeena turned the baby's head, eased its shoulders out, and suddenly he was fully there on the bed. He.

"It's a little boy," said Dick.

As soon as Wymeena clamped the umbilical cord, Dick and Wymeena helped Mariah roll onto her back and placed the baby on her chest. Dick looked at the baby with adoring eyes. "Mariah, he's beautiful!"

Mariah had her face turned away. Her chin quivered. "I'm afraid to see him."

"Just. Look. At. Him!"

She did. His eyes looked into hers, unfocused as they were. She saw trust. Her baby. Trusting her. Love swelled between them and enveloped the three.

"My family," said Mariah.

* * *

Acknowledgments

I am grateful to all who have supported and guided me through this creative process. My first supporter, Rev. Georgie Richardson, led me through many years of learning about manifestation and spiritual life. It would have been daunting to write this book without her encouragement. My first editor, Kay Derochie, taught me about those tricky verb tenses, among other things. I'm grateful to all my beta readers, who helped me see where my novel could be improved. A big thank you to Malcolm MacGregor for the beautiful picture of the entrance to Percy Warner Park. It was worth watching and waiting for you to finish walking the entire Appalachian trail to contact you for the license. At the top of my gratitude list is Andy Ellis, my friend, my coach, and my amazing editor. Working with Andy has kept the years-long work of revising and editing joyful. And last but not least, I thank my sweet husband, Wally, for putting up with this endeavor.